The Battlefield of
FAITH

The Battlefield of
FAITH

(THE FAITH SERIES BOOK 2)

A Seven Stage Reset for Wounded Clergy

Rev. Dr. Donald R. Hayes, DTh DMin

The Battlefield of Faith

Copyright © 2024 by Rev. Dr. Donald R. Hayes, DTh DMin. All rights reserved.

No part of this publication may be reproduced, stored in a retrieval system or transmitted in any way by any means, electronic, mechanical, photocopy, recording or otherwise without the prior permission of the author except as provided by USA copyright law.

The opinions expressed by the author are not necessarily those of URLink Print and Media.

1603 Capitol Ave., Suite 310 Cheyenne, Wyoming USA 82001
1-888-980-6523|admin@urlinkpublishing.com

URLink Print and Media is committed to excellence in the publishing industry.

Book design copyright © 2024 by URLink Print and Media. All rights reserved.

Published in the United States of America

Library of Congress Control Number: 2024904272
ISBN 978-1-68486-704-2 (Paperback)
ISBN 978-1-68486-709-7 (Digital)

23.01.24

CONTENTS

Preface vii

Dedication ix

Acknowledgements xi

Chapter One: Introduction 1

Chapter Two: The Biblical Basis For This Book 25

Chapter Three: Theaters of Conflict 74

Chapter Four: Proposed Clergy Care Retreat 105

Chapter Five: Why A Clergy Care Center Matters 133

Chapter Six: The Literature Review 152

Appendix 169

Bibliography 177

PREFACE

This book is a blueprint to aid in recovering and resetting wounded clergy on the verge of burnout, causing them to leave their ministries and not return. The decline of trained clergy for ministry labor is at an all-time high. Clerics from all Christian denominations are leaving their respective ministries at an alarming rate. This issue is a time bomb waiting to happen. If the Christian church does not acknowledge the problems and take corrective action, many generations of potential church members will fall by the wayside. Although there are similar retreats in place, there needs to be more. This book outlines an expense-free three-day retreat called Slains Ministries. A 501 (c) 3 Foundation and charitable contributions will underwrite the costs.

Five Protestant clerics were selected to provide expert personal revelations and suggestions on a healing ministry that would reduce the monthly exit of wounded ministers and return them to their churches renewed, refreshed, and restored. It is not a cure but a reset to begin the healing process and keep ministers in the field God called them to serve.

DEDICATION

To my wife, Cynthia, my soulmate, who has supported me in every call. God has led me from parish ministry to chaplaincy. You have been my rock and sounding board. You encouraged me when all seemed lost, and the mountain seemed too high, the valley too low, and the river too wide. Your love helped me endure the long hours of research and sleepless hours at the computer writing this blueprint for a healing ministry for the many clerics and families who needed this help.

ACKNOWLEDGEMENTS

I cannot express my profound appreciation to the faculty, staff, and administration of Erskine Theological Seminary and Dr. Loyd Melton for the opportunity to learn from some of the most gifted theologians of our time, including Dr. R. J. Gore, who have shared their cumulative experiences from decades of training clergy for the harvest. They helped me form the tenets of Slains Ministries in such a way as to make it a viable and likely ministry.

I want to express my appreciation to all my friends and family, especially my twin brother Ronnie, who journeyed with me along this spiritual path, always giving a kind word or message of hope. They share in the vision of Slains Ministries and the good it may bring to wounded clerics from every background and denomination.

I wish to thank the five clergymen, Rev. Dr. Kurtes Quisenberry, Rev. Kirby Winstead, Rev. Marshall Ivey, Rev. Elgin Woodberry, and Rev. Sam Boone, who gave their time and energy to help me navigate the battlefield where the work of ministry meets the road.

I am thankful for my spiritual trust and support team, including Sandy Springs, Dr. Buddy Witherspoon, Dr. Tom Mullikin, Bruce and Shirley Walters, Jumpmaster Johnny H. Smith, Dr. Charles Campbell, Phyllis J. Sheffer, Ronald L. Hayes, Jim Docherty—especially Dr. Kathleen Hines, who edited much of my material.

And, of course, my Lord and Savior, Jesus Christ, whom I am constantly reminded that I am nothing without Him.

CHAPTER ONE

An Introduction to the Book

The Need

Recent surveys have confirmed that Christian clerics have been leaving their respective ministries in record numbers. This problem has been brewing for decades but is now in crisis. These statistics show that their exit may be the tip of the iceberg since many go unreported. Often, the problem relates to burnout or job-related stress. Many more issues are undermining the effectiveness of Christian ministry. These issues will be detailed in t book with proposed solutions.

To curb this decline, this book is the basis for a proposed retreat that will be a pilot program for wounded clergy. The formulation will begin by designing a website, preparing job descriptions for future staff, developing treatment programs, and creating a board of directors. The board will set a policy to meet the requirements of a 501c3 tax-exempt foundation. This foundation will be made through the IRS.[1] In addition, a non-profit corporation through the South Carolina Secretary of State will be formed to underwrite the expenses of a paid three-day retreat[2]. Charitable donations from

---

[1] Jonathan Barry Forman, Roberta F. Mann, "Making the Internal Revenue Service Work." Fla. Tax Rev. 17 (2015): 725.

[2] Edward P. Harding, Jr., "Keeping the Connection: An Examination of the Perils and Benefits of a Church Connected 501c3 (Non-Profit) Corporation" (Ph.D.

public and private corporations and individual contributions will provide financial support. Grants from many local, state, and federal government agencies will increase the support. Slains Ministries will be introduced as a combined clinical and spiritual retreat where wounded clergy can reclaim and reset their unique ministries.

Ministers and laity have for decades trekked to Moncks Corner, South Carolina, along the banks of the Cooper River in Berkeley County to refresh and restore their wounded or tired spirits. While not designated as a healing retreat per se, Mepkin Abbey[3] is a place to refresh one's spirit. It is administered by Roman Catholic Trappist monks of the Cistercian Order who live in quiet harmony with nature. Daily, they commune with God in prayer, spiritual study, work, and hospitality. Their *modus operandi* requires them to remain void of speech while using sign language to communicate. In theory, they believe that one cannot hear God speak while speaking. Silence is a unique way to commune with God. Similarly, while not ascribing to silence alone, a healthy Slains Ministry will be designed to reset wounded ministers. It will comprise a three-day retreat that initially accommodates up to ten pastors and could increase over time.

There are numerous treatment centers in America addressing similar problems. However, they are devoted to other groups of individuals not necessarily related to the clergy. There is a need for more centers to meet the increasing demands of reset, restoration, and renewal. Many are designed for groups such as present or prior military personnel or victims of domestic abuse. Carefully evaluating the operation of these different centers will help develop a care plan for wounded pastors' needs and concerns.

The experiences of five pastors will also be included as a reference to clergies who have faced stress and burnout and survived to share their experiences. They will provide data from a questionnaire on issues that must be addressed. Their advice will help develop practical solutions and effective programs to help heal wounded clerics. Slains

---

diss., Hartford Seminary, 1993), ProQuest dissertations (9532791).

[3] "Mepkin Abbey," Mepkin Abbey, accessed September 21, 2022, https://www.mepkinabbey.org/.

Ministries is the vehicle that is designed as a pilot program to reset and restore clerics to the mission fields they were called to serve.

To underscore the need for this book, a few years ago, a young Anglican priest and his wife were serving the needs of a small church plant in Garden City[4], South Carolina. Forty-five church members gathered to establish a place of worship in a rented storefront. The priest was recruited to shepherd them with promises that, when the time came, they would provide a living wage for him and his family. This remuneration and medical and retirement benefits would provide the means to support his family and settle into that community. Six months passed, and by then, the church bank account had exceeded ten thousand dollars. So, the young priest asked the vestry to fulfill their pledge and begin paying him for services rendered.

When the request was initiated, the senior warden[5] replied, "We can't pay you a salary; we have a church to build!" The priest asked, "How can I provide for my family?" The senior warden stated emphatically, "That's God's department; he will provide for you." The priest answered, "Yes, and God will provide through the people of his church." The lines were drawn between the senior warden and the young priest. A second action materialized when the priest discovered that the senior warden had backchanneled to the bishop for several months, falsely reporting how unfit the young priest was to serve.

Soon the bishop summoned the priest and instructed him to return to Florida and begin retraining in parish administration. This weighed heavy on the priest's heart and led him to disassociate from this ecclesiastical jurisdiction and his local church. This story may not be a case of burnout, but it depicts job-related stress, pain, and suffering. The young priest and his family sequestered in their small den for three days, asking if parish ministry had been God's calling.

---

[4] Dean Thrift Sinclair, "A New Town Will Appear on Charleston Neck" (Ph.D. diss., Louisiana State University and Agricultural & Mechanical College, 2001), LSU Digital Commons (3042651).

[5] Robert Bolt, "Franklin Delano Roosevelt, Senior Warden, St. James Church at Hyde Park, New York," *Historical Magazine of the Protestant Episcopal Church*, 54 no. 1 (1985), 91-99.

Their family unit was injured, and their emotions were bruised. They grieved for their church family and never felt such deep pain. The priest and his wife contemplated leaving the ministry for another vocation. The pain and suffering caused by this senior warden, an officer of the church, caused a deep wound in the priest's soul, even taking the desire for service to God to the brink. He quipped, "Seminary did not prepare me for this painful situation."

This story is likely repeated numerous times across America by numerous clerics who face the same friction while serving the needs of their churches. Therefore, this book proposes to develop a pilot program for a retreat where the pastor can reconnect to his calling, family, church, and Creator. In doing so, the hope is that wounded pastors can find shalom and joy again. Thus, they will become whole again and rejoin in communion with God and their fellow believers.

The Process

A unique seven-stage process will be used. It is called the *Slains Seven-Stage Reset* and hopefully will lead to the reset, renewal, and restoration of clergies to their mission and naming. This overarching theme will guide the pilot program and the learning outcomes. These seven stages will lead the clergyman from the hills to the valleys and rise again like a "J" curve. This process is sequenced and designated as battlefields as follows: 1) Vanity/Pride, 2) Doubt/Depression, 3) Temptation/Addiction, 4) Guilt/Despair, 5) Fear/Anxiety, 6) Faith/Trust, and 7) Hope/Peace.

Stage one is the fall. Stages two through five are sequential results of the battlefields. Stage six becomes a landing zone or safety net, while stage seven represents the victory or reset. Stages two through five are aggressive battlefields, while stages six and seven are passive battlefields. They are the battlegrounds that will continue throughout a pastor's ministry. Stages six and seven are sources of strength and cement the reset process for the spiritual warrior who will constantly be at odds to keep stages one through five at bay. Stages one through five are battlegrounds that must remain defeated and stay in the lost category.

When clerics journey through these seven stages, the Slains Ministry team hopes that they will regain the joy for their respective ministries. These seven stages are interconnected in a circle of hope from man's fallen nature to his restoration, renewal, and recall of his ministry. These stages are the themes for the three-day retreat's morning and evening topics. They will underscore the therapies in these six sessions. The seventh stage, hope/peace, will be a bonus session provided as a handout or delivered on Friday morning's departure.

The Retreat

Although the future location of Slains Ministries is not yet determined, this three-day all-expense paid retreat could be on campus at The Anglican Church of the Advent in Marion, South Carolina. This church and parish hall is in Marion, S.C. It is a possible setting and laboratory to begin a ministry such as Slains Ministries. The sanctuary can hold as many as 120 worshippers. The adjacent parish hall includes a dining room as well as kitchen facilities. There are areas in the parish hall that could accommodate meeting rooms and individual counseling spaces. The parish hall already has tables, chairs, and a meeting lounge.

The Anglican Church of the Advent Marion occupies over one acre, so there is room to grow. It is envisioned that a residential building could be constructed to accommodate up to sixteen people with sleeping quarters, bathrooms, and showers. A dinette and lounge area, in addition to a washer and dryer room, is also a consideration for this facility.

In addition to location, other issues need to be considered. There is a need for human resources where job descriptions are identified. In this modern world of communication, it is imperative to connect via the internet, so a website needs to be developed. Brochures must be created to send to prospective clergies needing Slains Ministries services. A board of directors must oversee the legal and accounting departments. This is just the tip of the iceberg. There will be many more needs before Slains becomes a reality.

There are some obstacles to Slains Ministries. Foremost is solving the problem of wounded ministers who have experienced post-traumatic stress disorder (PTSD)[6]. Wounded pastors suffering from trauma and having left their churches are not inclined to visit church property because of the bad memories associated with a place of worship. Building Slains Ministries on church property may or may not be a thoughtful decision. Perhaps a neutral location would better serve the needs of wounded pastors and Slains Ministries. Many choices are necessary to move this pilot project forward, but miracles can happen in prayer and with God leading the way.

When Slains Ministries begins operations, an executive director will oversee the day-to-day operations. This executive will follow the guidance of the board of directors who manage the 501(c)3 foundation. They will approve and manage the training and curriculum of the staff who administer the treatment plans. The board will lead in raising the monies needed to pay for the tuition and expenses for the program. The only cost for those who attend will be the travel to and from to attend the three-day retreat.

This book speaks to the social and spiritual needs of the clergy. This ministry of healing requires an environment with as few distractions as possible. As Abigail Van Buren said, 'The church is a hospital for sinners, not a sanctuary for saints.'[7] While weekly Sunday worship service is helpful and necessary for the laity and clergy, when events in the life of clergy become untenable, there is a strong need for a period of rest and spiritual renewal through a structured and more in-depth place of healing.

Expected Outcomes

The specific learning outcomes for clergy who attend Slains Ministries' three-day retreat are not feasible at this point and would

---

[6] Nancy C. Andreasen. "What is Post-Traumatic Stress Disorder?" (01 APR 2022), 240-243. https://www.tandfonline.com/doi/full/10.31887/DCNS.2011.13.2/nandreasen.

[7] "Abigail Van Buren Quotes," *Goodreads*, accessed October 31, 2022, https://www.goodreads.c/quotes.

otherwise be made through subjective reasoning. A quantitative effect cannot be projected until this proposal is developed and the operation is functional. However, five clerics have been assembled to discuss the treatment programs that could be most helpful for wounded clergy. These pastors have in common the wounds of clerics from their respective ministries. They will offer insight to other clergy facing similar burnout, rejection, and disinterest in their calling and describe how they recovered to reclaim their ministries.

These clerics will shed light on experiences such as a) Have I begun the road to recovery? b) Do I want to continue in my present ministry? c) Do I want to look at alternate ministries where I can fulfill the tenets of my calling? d) Has my spirit been restored where I can look forward to serving my master and doing so joyfully? e) Have I found shalom and peace moving forward?

The following corporate goals are worth considering for the Slains Ministry team: a) Did we curb, arrest, or slow down the downward spiral of many of these clerics who are having trouble with their cognitive, emotional, and spiritual affairs? b) Did we set these clerics on a path to restoration and renewal? c) Did we successfully reconnect these pastors to their ministries, families, and church? d) Can we confidently send them back into the fight for the hearts and souls of the congregations they serve? e) Do we recommend that this minister look for another expression of his ministry apart from the experience he has had for so long? There are multiple ministries where one can serve. Hospitals, hospices, the military, first responders, chaplaincy, and educational institutions are other places where a minister can apply his experience and expertise.

The learning outcomes will be based on the curriculum and training resources used to equip the Slains Ministries Clergy Retreat participants. Much of this material is in the developmental stages, where the bulk of the research will be centered as this proposal unfolds. There is no desire to reinvent the wheel or rewrite successful materials available online and in academic institutions. However, if the research creates a new approach to improve counseling and treatment sessions, this data will be provided as determined by the board of directors. Slains Ministries envisions providing as many valuable results as possible or professional aphorisms at little or no cost to anyone interested in helping wounded clergy reset and reclaim their calling.

Goals for Slains Ministries

The following goals are as follows:

- To effectively ascertain and analyze the phenomena of clergy burnout and work-related stress: their causes, effects, and the most prevalent associated problems.
- To understand, through interviews with five clergy members from different backgrounds, the personal effects of burnout and job-related stress are the most pressing issues that must be addressed.
- Through an extensive literature review, discover and analyze what programs have been developed to address clergy job-related stress, ascertain the most effective treatments, and create an effective program for a three-day retreat in Slains Ministries.

Statistical Crisis

The spark that brought this concept to the forefront was a 2021 survey conducted by The Fuller Institute, George Barna Group, Lifeway, Schaeffer Institute of Leadership Development, *Christianity Today*, and Pastoral Care, Inc.[8] Chief among the findings was the statistic that 1500 clergy leave the pulpit every month. Four thousand new churches begin each year, while 7000 churches close yearly. Over 1300 pastors were terminated by the local church each month, many

---

[8] "Statistics for Pastors," Pastoral Care, Inc., accessed December 1, 2022, https://www.pasotralcareomc.com.

without cause. It is unclear if this number is included in the 1500 clergy leaving each month. In the newly revised statistics:

> Thirty-eight percent of pastors are thinking of quitting the ministry,
> Fifty-one percent from mainline denominations (November 29, 2021).
> Of the fifty-one percent, almost half (forty-six percent) are under forty-five.
> Fifty percent of pastors are now of the age of fifty-six and above.
> Seventy-two percent of pastors report working between fifty-five to seventy-five hours per week.
> Eighty-four percent of pastors feel they are on call twenty-four/seven.
> Eighty percent believe pastoral ministry has negatively affected their families. Many pastors' children do not attend church now because of what the church has done to their parents.
> Sixty-five percent of pastors feel their family lives in a "glass house" and fear they are not good enough to meet expectations.
> Twenty-three percent of pastors report being distant from their families.
> Seventy-eight percent of pastors report having their vacation and personal time interrupted by ministry duties and expectations.
> Sixty-five percent of pastors feel they have not spent enough vacation with their families over the last five years.
> Twenty-eight percent of pastors report feeling guilty for taking personal time off and not telling the church.

Thirty-five percent of pastors report that the demands of the church deny them from spending time with their families.

Twenty-four percent of pastors' families resent the church and its effect on their families.

Twenty-two percent of pastors' spouses report that the ministry places undue expectations on their families.

Sixty-six percent of church members expect a minister and family to live by a higher moral standard than themselves.

Fifty-three percent of pastors report that the seminary did not prepare them for the ministry.

Ninety percent of pastors report that the ministry was completely different from what they thought it would be before they entered it.

Forty-five percent of pastors spend ten-fifteen hours a week on sermon preparation.

Ninety-five percent of pastors report not praying daily or regularly with their spouses.

Fifty-seven percent of pastors believe they do not receive a livable wage.

Fifty-seven percent of pastors report not being able to pay their bills.

Fifty-three percent of pastors are concerned about their future family's financial security.

Seventy-five percent of pastors report significant stress-related crises at least once in their ministry.

Eighty percent of pastors and eighty-four percent of their spouses have felt unqualified and discouraged as role models at least once or more in their ministries.

Fifty-two percent of pastors feel overworked and cannot meet their church's unrealistic expectations.

Fifty-four percent of pastors find the role of a pastor overwhelming.

Forty percent reported severe conflict with a parishioner at least once last year.

Eighty percent of pastors expect conflict within their church.

Seventy-five percent of pastors report spending four-five hours weekly in needless meetings.

Thirty-five percent of pastors battle depression or fear of inadequacy.

Twenty-six percent of pastors report being overfatigued.

Twenty-eight percent of pastors report they are spiritually undernourished.

Over fifty percent of pastors state that the biggest challenge is to recruit volunteers and encourage their members to change (living closer to God's Word).

Seventy percent of pastors report a lower self-image than when they first started.

Seventy percent of pastors do not have someone they consider to be a close friend.

Twenty-seven percent of pastors report not having anyone to turn to for help in a crisis.

Eighty-one percent of pastors have been tempted to have inappropriate sexual thoughts or behavior with someone in the church but have resisted.

Seventeen percent of pastors report inappropriately texting with a church member at some time in their ministry.

Thirty-four percent of pastors wrestle with the temptation of pornography or visit pornographic sites.

Fifty-seven percent of pastors feel fulfilled yet discouraged, stressed, and fatigued.

Eighty-four percent of pastors desire a close fellowship with someone they can trust and confide in.

Over fifty percent of pastors are unhealthy, overweight, and do not exercise.

The profession of "pastor" is near the bottom of a survey of the most-respected trades, just above "car salesman."

Many denominations are reporting an "empty Pulpit Crisis." They do not have a shortage of ministers but lack ministers desiring to fill the role of a pastor.

Seventy-one percent of churches have no plan for a pastor to receive a periodic sabbatical.

Sixty-six percent of churches have no lay counseling support.

Thirty percent of churches have no documentation clearly outlining what the church expects of their pastor.

One out of every ten pastors will retire as a pastor.

The Gallup poll states that there has been a ten-point drop in church attendance from the previous decade.

Forty-five percent of American adults say they attend religious services, an all-time low.

Fifty percent of Americans state they are members of a church.

Thirty-six percent say they have confidence in the church or organized religion.

According to Lifeway, six out of ten churches are plateaued or have declining attendance. More than half of their churches (Baptist) saw fewer than ten people who became Christians in the last twelve months[9].

In *Clergy Burnout,* author Fred Lehr reports on a study conducted by the Fuller Theological Seminary in the late 1980s, giving a notable contrast to the 2021 survey by Pastoral Care, Inc. In it, he says the following:

> Ninety percent of pastors work more than forty-six hours per week.
> Eighty percent believe that pastoral ministry is affecting their families negatively.
> Thirty-three percent say that "being in ministry is a hazard to my family."
> Seventy-five percent have reported significant crises due to stress at least once in their ministry.
> Fifty percent felt unable to meet the needs of the ministry.
> Ninety percent felt they were not adequately trained to cope with the ministry demands placed upon them.
> Forty percent reported one serious conflict with at least one parishioner at least once a month.
> Seventy percent of pastors do not have someone they would consider a close friend.
> Thirty-seven percent admitted engaging in inappropriate sexual behavior with someone in their congregation.
> Seventy percent have a lower self-image after they have been in pastoral ministry than when they start.

---

[9] Edited by Frank Newport. The Gallop Poll Public Opinion 2009 (New York: Rowman & Littlefield Publishers, Inc., 2009), Introduction.

These statistics show that fifty clergy members will leave their respective ministries for another vocation before the sun goes down on this day. This is alarming and should be a clarion call for reasonable minds to form an army of caring professionals who can stymie this decline for no reason other than to stabilize clergy ranks. Many in active ministry bear witness to these statistics. Yet, there is hope in the power of healing from above.

Slains Ministries is being developed as a combined clinical and spiritual retreat where wounded clergy can reclaim and reset their ministry calling. The Christian church faces daunting problems, including challenges to church theology and dogma, method of worship, and church authority and discipline. Churches are formed by their seminaries and led by their clerics. Yet, when they succumb to the challenges of their office and find they can no longer function, it is time for a change. It is time to be refreshed, renewed, and reset.

Some say the church is entering a new dark age, increasing the challenges for today's Christian clergy. In *Clergy Burnout: Surviving in Turbulent Times*, author Fred Lehr says:

> We are facing a massive shift in our culture. In her book, The Great Emergence, Phyllis Tickle documents that Christianity undergoes a significant cultural change every five hundred years. Well, it has been five hundred years since the Reformation. It is time for a significant cultural shift. As if that were not enough, people in the United States and many places worldwide are dealing with a pandemic, an economic crisis, severe cultural and social movements such as Black Lives Matter and LGBTQIA+ and gender equality efforts, climate change, and more. These are all critical challenges and worthy of our attention. The pandemic alone is enough to send

The Battlefield of Faith

> our world, including the world of congregational ministry, in a dither.[10]

This passage underscores the great difficulties of society, the church, and the clerics called upon to lead congregations in instruction from the Word of God. The prophet Isaiah writes, "In the wilderness, prepare the way of the Lord; make straight in a desert highway for our God."

The Protestant Reformation began an upheaval in the Catholic Church. It addressed many errors of the organized church. The reforms had a lasting effect and were a significant improvement. However, the loss of hierarchal authority may be the least effective result of the movement. It opened the door for believers of different religious views to proliferate unabated, establishing new followings and denominations under the umbrella of Christianity. The mainline Protestant denominations have proved their worth, but the ensuing splinter groups have steered far from the tenets of the Christian faith as expressed by the Apostles Creed.

CHANGE AND CONFLICT

Christians are in a time of change and conflict, according to Marcus J. Borg. In *The Heart of Christianity: Rediscovering a Life of Faith*, Borg says, "Christians in North America today are deeply divided about the heart of Christianity. We live in a time of major conflict in the church. Millions of Christians are embracing an emerging way of seeing Christianity's heart. Millions of other Christians continue to embrace an earlier vision of Christianity, often defending it as traditional Christianity and the only legitimate way of being a Christian."[11] Borg underscores Phyllis Tickle's[12] treatise

---

[10] Fred Lehr, *Clergy Burnout: Surviving in Turbulent Times, Revised and Expanded*. (Minneapolis: Fortress Press, 2022), Preface.

[11] Marcus J. Borg, *The Heart of Christianity: Rediscovering A Life Of Faith* (New York: Harper One, 2003), 2.

[12] Phyllis Tickle, *The Great Emergence: How Christianity is Changing and Why* (Kentwood: Baker Books, 2012), Preface.

that the Christian church is in a period of change and conflict, which occurs about every five hundred years. Clerics are trying to navigate this changing world where Christianity is being redefined. Ultimately, this places clerics in the middle, where they are expected to choose one side. This is not a comfortable place to live or exist.

This "No-Man's-Land"[13] is Brian D. McLaren's description in *A New Kind of Christianity – Ten Questions That Are Transforming the Faith*, where many clerics find themselves. He says,

> My theology seemed to unravel a little more every month for several years. I was afraid nothing would soon be left—which is unsettling, especially when you make your living as a pastor. I remember taking long walks alone, praying, thinking, and wondering what would happen if better answers never came. I could not think of anyone with whom I could share my deep agony. It was a scary and challenging time.[14]

These raw thoughts reveal the hearts of ministers today and mirror the days of Jesus Christ. McLaren describes lonely walks in prayer and meditation and feeling like there was no one to turn to with his innermost thoughts of fear, anxiety, and, more than likely, his calling to be a pastor. This is evidence of why there is a great need for a place of healing or reset, such as Slains Ministries.

This need for healing is seen in how the importance of the American church is declining:

> A new report by Pew Research Center and the General Social Survey published Tuesday (September 13, 2022) found a surge of adults leaving Christianity to become atheist, agnostic,

---

[13] "No Man's Land," Merriam-Webster, accessed November 30, 2022, https://www.merriam-webster.com/dictionary/no-man%27s-land.

[14] Brian D. McLaren, *A New Kind of Christianity – Ten Questions That Are Transforming the Faith* (New York: Harper One, 2010), 6.

The Battlefield of Faith

or 'nothing in particular. It predicted that if the number of Christians under 30 abandoning their faith accelerates beyond the current pace, adherents of the historically dominant religion of the U.S. could become a minority by 2045.[15]

This book reported that the percentage of Americans who identified as Christians in the early 1990s was 90 percent, including children. This number had fallen to 64 percent by 2020. It was discovered that Judaism, Hinduism, Islam, and Buddhism represented 6 percent of the U.S. population in 2020. The number of Americans without religious affiliation nearly doubled from 16 percent to 29 percent in 2020.

These startling statistics do not bode well for Christianity moving forward. However, it may be an opportunity for a looming revival of traditional Christian practices and worship. Yet, the decline of Americans identifying as Christian becomes an added burden for wounded clergy. It makes it more challenging to maintain their ministries and keep them thriving and healthy. This situation poses a dilemma for people of faith. Given such daunting statistics, is anyone wondering why so many clerics leave the church each month? The facts underscore the challenge.

Sadly, the pandemic has made this situation much worse. All studies note that an unprecedented number of Protestant pastors are considering quitting the ministry, the Barna Group says. "Since before the pandemic, Barna has been tracking worship shifting and the uncertain digital and physical realities of churches in America. As the pandemic era accelerated the reality of a new Sunday morning, many pastors have asked, 'What is going on with church attendance?'"[16]

---

[15] Jon Brown, "Nearly One-third of Churches Split from Regional Methodist Church Body Amid Ongoing Schism About Sexuality," *Fox News*, accessed January 10, 2023, https://www.foxnews.com/us/nearly-one-third-churches-split-regional-methodist-church-body-amid-ongoing-schism-about-sexuality.

[16] "A New Chapter in Millennial Church Attendance. Articles in Faith & Christianity," Barna Group, accessed December 10, 2022, https://barna.com/research.

Additionally, the poll revealed that the burnout rate among pastors had risen exponentially over the past few years, reporting 42 percent of pastors wondering if they should abandon their vocation altogether. That number marked an increase of 13 percent since Barnas's similar poll in January 2021, when just 29 percent felt that way. These pastors named stress (56 percent), loneliness (43 percent), and political divisions (38 percent) as the top reasons they have become weary of the job, as well as the toll it has taken on their families (29 percent). And "Pastors have considered quitting full-time ministry because the cumulative effect wears on the soul."[17] Pastors are battling burnout amid politics, the Covid-19 pandemic, and American youth abandoning their faith for atheism or agnosticism, or no religious affiliation.

The Battle

This book is entitled *The Battlefield of Faith* and introduces a retreat christened Slains Ministries. It is a pilot program where clergy can refresh, restore, and renew their ministries. The focus of this pilot program is to provide healing for wounded clerics who need a reset.

One of the many difficulties of this pilot program is that not all clerics are equal, especially in terms of denominational doctrine and worship. The expected participants in Slains Ministries will arrive from all backgrounds and theological perspectives. They will bring views and prejudices to the retreat that others will not share, such as methods of baptism or, once saved, always saved ideas of theology. The realm of theological opinions and disciplines varies as far as the East is from the West. However, Jesus called for unity, and Slains Ministries' desire is for clerics from all Christian denominations to set their differences aside and focus on restoring their ministries and calling.

---

[17] Jon Brown. "Nearly One-Third of Churches Split From Regional Methodist Church Body Amid Ongoing Schism About Sexuality," *Fox News*, accessed January 10, 2023, https://www.foxnews.com/us/nearly-one-third-churches-split-regional-methodist-church-body-amid-ongoing-schism-about-sexuality.

The Battlefield of Faith

It will be incumbent on the staff and leaders of Slains Ministries to minimize denominational differences and look at the servant of God through the eyes of the Creator. Thus, an effort to maximize the Christian faith and calling will be the thread that ties all clerics together. This is how Slains Ministries will look at the wounded and burned-out clerics who find their way to this retreat.

Reasonable use of military language will be utilized to highlight the inherent challenges in this pilot program, just as Jesus Christ often used symbolic terminology. Christ often used biblical symbols like a shepherd to his sheep to symbolize a pastor about his congregation. The image we see will be the battlefield. New Spring Church provides an article about the fight between good and evil as spiritual warfare. In the article, it is written, "Satan is real. Just under the surface of everyday interactions, hiding in the shadows clouded in mystery and confusion, the devil works to undermine what God is doing in us and through us. Angels, demons, spiritual warfare—they all exist, but we do not have to live in fear of the supernatural."[18]

Perhaps burnout and job-related stress are alarming because countless clerics are called to a lifelong vocation but are no longer in God's service. These spiritual warriors in God's army were trained leaders equipped to engage the evil in this world. Losing these highly trained soldiers is unacceptable for those whose ranks are growing thinner daily. Clergy and laity must be refreshed, and their hearts renewed to extend the battlefield of faith. The ability to engage the enemy in this battle for the lost is a noble calling. Newly minted seminarians quickly find that they need thick skin to survive the work they are called to do.

Paul instructs clerics, laymen, and women on the road to sanctification, as he writes in the letter to the Ephesians 6:10-13:

> Finally, be strong in the Lord and his mighty power. Put on God's whole armor to stand against the devil's schemes. Our struggle

---

[18] "10 Bible Verses on Spiritual Warfare," New Spring Church, accessed December 12, 2022, https://newspring.cc/articles/10-scriptures-on-spiritual-warfare.

is not against flesh and blood but the powers of this dark world and the spiritual forces of evil in the heavenly realms. Therefore, put on the whole armor of God so that when the day of evil comes, you may be able to stand your ground after you have done everything to stand.

This book aims to develop a retreat where pastors from all Christian denominations can begin to reconnect to their calling, their families, their churches, and their Creator. This pilot program is not a cure but a reset of the pastor's journey to find fulfillment in their ministry.

Additionally, an examination of the current state of the church and its clerics must include how it arrived at this situation to fully understand the dilemma of spiritual warfare and its adverse effects on clergy and their families. As in any combat situation, there are casualties of war. Often, the spouses and children of pastors suffer collateral damage or unintended consequences that sometimes lead to irreparable damage, such as estrangement or marital divorce.

Slains Ministries desires to help prevent divorce among clerics and help families injured because of their relationship with the pastor. If this ministry can mitigate these spiritual casualties, then the pastor can more quickly reset, restore, and renew. This pilot program aims to address the spiritual needs of the clerics. Then, we will look for ways to curb the decline, remove it, and replace it with positive results.

Clerics battle for the hearts, minds, and souls of the lost and, in turn, the faithful. This requires clergy to be vigilant because "Evil stalks the children of the light in a dark world."[19] The world lessens the impact of evil in the minds of everyone and makes the devil a hero-like figure. This mitigates the danger lurking in our midst. Jesus

---

[19] Eph. 5:7-14.

The Battlefield of Faith

Christ knew the inherent risk and made known the awareness and need to be aware in The Lord's Prayer[20], as follows:

> Our Father in Heaven,
> Hallowed be your name,
> Your kingdom come,
> Your will be done on earth as it is in heaven.
> Give us today our daily bread.
> And forgive us our debts,
> as we also have forgiven our debtors.
> And lead us not into temptation,
> But deliver us from the evil one.

The last line in this prayer underscores the importance of being aware of evil. It directs clergy to focus on the presence of sin and its destructive nature upon all people, including believers and nonbelievers. Jesus said, "Those who are well do not need a physician, but those who are sick."[21] Society and the world have worked overtime to reimage evil as nothing more than a make-believe figure or a close friend. The devil is annually the center of attention on Halloween, with his supposed likeness in costumes for every age. Society has caricatured the devil as a red-colored demon with horns, a three-pronged spear, and a pointed tail. Although this is a picture of evil, it is misleading because sin is far more deceptive and addictive.

Hollywood[22] movies render evil in horror films, but viewing the results of sin and living its terrifying results are different. Although movies broadcast evil as entertainment, it is nothing to emulate or adore. Evil is destructive and causes pain of every kind. This last admonishment by Jesus Christ receives little attention but has the

---

[20] Matt: 6:9-13.
[21] Matt 9:12.
[22] Allen John Scott, *On Hollywood: The Place, the Industry* (Princeton: Princeton University Press, 2005), 22.

most effect on everyone. Sin is addressed in Psalm 23 as well, where it is written:

1. The Lord is my Shepherd; I shall not want.
2. He maketh me to lie down in green pastures; he leadeth me beside the still waters.
3. He restoreth my soul; he leadeth me in the paths of righteousness for His name's sake.
4. Yea, though I walk through the valley of the shadow of death, I will fear no evil; for thou art with me; thy rod and thy staff they comfort me.
5. Thou preparest a table before me in the presence of my enemies; thou anointest my head with oil; my cup runneth over.
6. Surely goodness and mercy shall follow me all the days of my life, and I will dwell in the house of the Lord forever.

The verse, "Yea, though I walk through the valley of the shadow of death," references evil and the devil. The journey for clergy is through this valley. The shadow of death is all around. This is another sign of being aware of evil while it stalks everyone, especially clergy on the frontlines of the war of good versus evil. This is another validation of the importance of having a place of rest and respite in the name of Slains Ministries.

Book Structure

The structure of this book gains its footing in the following illustration of an opportunity to envision and rebuild the church, one parish, and one priest at a time. As Cardinal Avery Dulles writes, "Jesus continues to shape the community of the faithful by word and sacrament."[23] This means that the structure or foundation of Slains Ministries will always be grounded on God's Word and the

---

[23] Cardinal Avery Dulles, Models of the Church (New York: Doubleday, 1978), 206.

Sacraments' practice, like Holy Communion, where Jesus said, "Do this in remembrance of Me."[24] The book will begin with the preface, dedication and acknowledgments followed by the six chapters, appendix and bibliography.

Chapter One is divided into five subheads: The Need, The Retreat, Expected Outcomes, The Present Crisis, The Battle, and The Structure of This Book. The Need begins with an introduction of recent surveys identifying issues facing clergies causing them to leave their respective ministries. It is followed by an example of a young priest who experienced job-related stress. It is one of many reasons clerics leave their churches in record numbers, including burnout.

The Retreat makes a case for developing a pilot project where clerics can attend a three-day all-expense paid retreat to face the challenges that are diminishing their ministries and provides steps to mitigate them. This subhead introduces Slains Ministries Seven Step Reset to fulfill that mission objective. Expected Outcomes will provide goals and objectives for Slains Ministries. The Present Crisis describes the church's challenges and problems facing clerics and their families. This subhead includes a valuable and alarming survey of the current state of church affiliation, disaffiliation, and various difficulties that all denominations face. The Battle subhead provides the range of the battlefield in terms of good versus evil.

In the book of Ecclesiasticus is written God gives man a choice between water and fire. There is no middle ground where the world wants everyone to be. The last subhead is The Structure of This Book which highlights the summary of each chapter in this book.

Chapter Two will examine the biblical basis for developing a retreat for wounded clergy. It will summarize the Slains Seven-Stage Reset of 1) Pride/Vanity, 2) Doubt/Depression, 3) Temptation/Addiction, 4) Guilt/Despair, 5) Fear/Anxiety, 6) Faith/Trust, and 7) Hope/Peace. Each stage will be underpinned by the biblical/theological foundations for retreats and how God uses brokenness to strengthen wounded clerics for parish ministries. Various Biblical texts will be examined with an accompanying commentary.

---

[24] 1 Cor. 11:24.

Chapter Three will analyze possible future conflicts and offer solutions where the clerics can prepare for the battles ahead. Theaters of Conflict take shape in many forms and sizes, some seen and some unseen. These seven theaters will correlate with the Seven Stages of Reset.

Chapter Four will describe the plan of action, retreat details, and comparisons to other organizations providing similar treatment and solutions for clerics who have experienced burnout and a crisis in ministry.

Chapter Five will surmise the life experiences of five clerics who have experienced burnout in their respective churches and how they managed to survive those difficult times. This chapter seeks insight into the problems clerics face and hopes those dark days will have a brighter future.

Chapter Six will be the literature review, followed by the bibliography.

CHAPTER TWO

The Biblical Basis For This Book

COMMENTARIES

This chapter will provide a biblical basis for creating a respite center for wounded clergy. It is a roadmap to the many challenges clergy will face throughout their ministries. It is divided into seven parts or stages that outline the struggles that cause clergy to leave their professions. Each section will include several Biblical verses with a commentary on how it relates to that stage.

Famed Christian apologist C. S. Lewis says:

> The world is a dance in which good, descending from God, is disturbed by evil arising from creatures, and the resulting conflict is resolved by God's assumption of the suffering nature that evil produces. The doctrine of the free Fall asserts that evil, which thus makes the fuel or raw material for the second and more complex kind of good, is not God's contribution but man's . . . Our present condition is explained by the fact that we are members of a spoiled

species. I do not mean that our sufferings are a punishment for being what we cannot now help being nor that we are morally responsible for the rebellion of a remote ancestor. If, nonetheless, I call our present condition one of Original Sin and not merely one of original misfortune, that is because our actual religious experience does not allow us to regard it in any other way.[25]

In many ways, the burden of clergy mirrors the lives of their parishioners, who attend Sunday worship services to find relief from their troubles. The crux of this study is based on the theory that many church members often unload their cares, needs, and concerns on their pastors. If the pastor is worth his weight in gold, he will journey with his troubled flock until their burdens are relieved. The catch is that now the pastor carries not only the parishioners' burdens but also his obligations and stresses. So where does the pastor find relief from the troubles inherited, which are added to his own? Slains Ministries will help ministers find relief from the weight of their calling and reset them for their continued labors in building the kingdom of God.

Gary McIntosh and Samuel Rima say in *Overcoming the Dark Side of Leadership*:

> In today's evangelical subculture, it seems that the answer to the question, what does it mean to act like a Christian? It is increasingly at odds with the teaching of Scripture. From both within and without, Christian leaders face a confusing and expansive menu of expectations when it comes to being a spiritual leader. Like the liturgists and mainline denominations that we readily accuse of being overly burdened

---

[25] Clive Staples Lewis, *The Problem of Pain* (New York: HarperCollins Publishers, 1996), 80-81

by human traditions, we have developed our expectations and spiritual standards of measure not entirely supported by the Scripture we hold so high. Our legalism is well-intended; nevertheless, it is repressive and destructive for those who must live and lead under its weight. Too many Christian leaders have forgotten the Reformation's liberating cry of 'sola Scriptura.' Like the Galatians of old, we may be guilty of trying to attain our holiness through human effort and regulations rather than through the sanctifying work of the Holy Spirit within us.[26]

Hence, the church faces mounting problems, including divisive challenges to its theology and dogma, method of worship, authority, and discipline. Some say the church is entering a new dark age, increasing the challenges for today's clergy. However, these problems are not new. In his day, Charles Spurgeon (1834-1892), a Baptist minister from England, stated, "One reason why the church of God at this moment has so little influence over the world is that the world has so much influence over the church."[27]

Newspaper and magazine headlines regularly report that churches of all denominations have declined, including the loss of clergy. The Covid-19 pandemic has accelerated this process. This exodus is a clarion call for the concept of a relief center. Although some recovery and support systems are in place, many more are necessary to meet the needs to restore the wounded servant and help him reclaim his calling.

The impact of this dilemma is far-reaching in all denominational communities but can be mitigated if spiritually healthy systems were

---

[26] Gary L. McIntosh and Samuel D. Rima, *Overcoming the Dark Side of Leadership: How to become an Effective Leader by Confronting Potential Failures*, revised edition (Grand Rapids: Baker Books, 2007), 183.

[27] Jarred Edgecomb, "*Spurgeon on Worldliness in the Church.*" Faithlife Sermons, accessed September 11, 2022, https://sermons.faithlife.com/sermons/89943-spurgeon-on-worldliness-in-the-church.

made available to ward off this ever-increasing problem. Leadership and stewardship only succeed when faithful people attempt to conduct worship services with their ministry leaders. This study will offer a proposed program to help clergy rekindle their calling. The vehicle to begin this startup is called Slains Ministries. When fully developed, it is desired that pastors will reset in such a way as to benefit the church for years to come.

The biblical basis for this study has as its foundation the words of Jesus Christ, who said: "The harvest is plentiful, but the laborers are few; therefore, pray earnestly to the Lord of the harvest to send out laborers into his harvest."[28] The phrase "The workers are few" is a tacit argument that no wounded clergy should be left behind. Every effort should be made to refresh, restore, and renew the wounded clergy and prepare the laborer for a return to the harvest. Christ reminds us in the Gospel of Matthew, "Come to me, all who are weary and heavy laden, and I will give your rest. Take my yoke upon you, and learn from me, for I am gentle and lowly in heart, and you will find rest for your souls. For my yoke is easy, and my burden is light."[29] This study aims to develop a blueprint for a place of respite to reclaim, reconnect, and reset the pastor's mission to serve God.

Again, in *Overcoming the Dark Side of Leadership,* authors Gary L. McIntosh and Samuel D. Rima say:

> As the baby boomers ascended to leadership roles, they carried their various dysfunctions. Most tragically fallen Christian leaders during the past ten to fifteen years have been baby boomers who felt driven to achieve and succeed in an increasingly competitive and demanding church environment. Their ambition has often been a subtle and dangerous combination of their dysfunctional personal needs and a certain measure of an altruistic desire to expand the

---

[28] Matt. 9:37-38.
[29] Matt. 11:28.

kingdom of God. However, because ambition is easily disguised in Christian circles and couched in the spiritual language (the need to fulfill the Great Commission and expand the church), the dysfunctions that drive Christian leaders often go undetected and unchallenged until it is too late.[30]

As Paul writes in Ephesians, "For our struggle is not against flesh and blood, but against the rulers, against the authorities, against the powers of this dark world and the spiritual forces of evil in the heavenly realms."[31] Thus, our clerics are spiritual warriors. Unlike their military counterparts, spiritual warriors wage war against the world, the flesh, and the devil. The difference is that these warriors battle in the spiritual realm, while military warriors fight in the realm of the mind and body. Like many military battles, the fighting is fierce. Soldiers grow weary, so military and spiritual warriors must step aside and recharge their batteries. Reclaiming the hearts, minds, and souls of the lost and lonely is daunting. It is compounded by the need to reclaim the downtrodden, neglected, abused, and abandoned.

For these rejected and canceled clergy, there is a biblical basis for this book where Peter states, "As you come to him, a living stone rejected by men but in the sight of God chosen and precious, you are like living stones being built as a spiritual house, to be a holy priesthood, to offer spiritual sacrifices acceptable to God through Jesus Christ."[32] Rejection by and in this world is inevitable because clerics are called to work where evil is lord. Clerics, like living stones, need to be built up. It is a reminder that a place for refreshment and renewal is part and parcel of service to the Church.

Isaiah exhorts, "He was wounded for our transgressions. He was bruised for our iniquities: The chastisement for our peace was upon Him, and by His stripes, we are healed."[33] As Chris DeRoco echoes, "Jesus's death on the cross healed us or delivered us from

---

[30] McIntosh and Rima, *Overcoming the Dark Side of Leadership*, 15.
[31] Eph. 6:12.
[32] 1 Pet. 2:4-5.
[33] Isa. 53:5.

the punishment of our sins in the past. He is now in the process of delivering us from the power of sin in the present."[34] The Bible teaches that the root of man's troubles is connected to sin. Paul writes of the flesh being at war with the spirit, and since unrepented sin hinders us all, it is an additional weight for the minister. It causes a separation from God, initiating a downward spiral, and the weight on the spiritual leader causes great suffering.

Slains Ministries is earmarked as the umbrella organization where wounded warriors can step aside to be refreshed and return, galvanized to continue in God's service. This renewal process is supported by a unique clinical therapy called the *Seven-Stage Reset* program. It is an original program developed to help restore and reset the wounded warrior. It is rooted in the seven deadly sins[35] of pride, greed, lust, envy, gluttony, wrath, and sloth.

Since the most potent mortal sin is pride, we are reminded in Proverbs 16:18 that "Pride goes before destruction and a haughty spirit before a fall. Better to be humble with the lowly than to divide the spoil with the proud."[36] An argument can be made about whether pride is the source of burnout or job-related stress. However, if pride were not present, there would be no need for Slains Ministries Retreat Center.

In his Sermon on the Mount, Christ reinforces the words in Peter when He says, "Blessed are you when others revile you, persecute you, and falsely utter all kinds of evil against you on my account. Rejoice and be glad; your reward is great in heaven, for they persecuted the prophets before you."[37] Ultimately, these are words of comfort for the injured spiritual warrior. No one likes conflict, but

---

[34] Chris DeRoco, *By His Stripes We Are Healed: Meaning and Importance of Isaiah 53:5*, Christianity.com, accessed September 12, 2022, https://www.christianity.com/wiki/bible/isaiah-53-5-says-by-his-stripes-we-are-healed-so-are-christians-freed-from-all-sickness.html.

[35] *Encyclopedia Britannica, Seven Deadly Sins: Definition, History, Names, & Examples*, accessed October 23, 2022, https://britannica.com/topic/seven-deadly-sins.

[36] Prov. 16:18-19.

[37] Matt. 5: 11-12.

individuals find they are called to engage the enemy of God, whether as warriors or as a support community.

There are many examples in the Bible concerning spiritual help for clerics who have reached a turning point in their respective ministries. Slains Ministries offers a place of healing, restoration, and reset--the desired outcome of this retreat concept. However, full recovery may take several years to complete. Slains Ministries is where clerics can stop the downward spiral of burnout[38] and other work-related breaking points.

This chapter will examine the seven stages or battlefields where clerics wage war with the spirit and mind. These seven stages culminate from years of clinical study, and the author determines their sequence. They have not been vetted nor validated by peer review. However, that process is expected to begin later when this Reset Therapy is offered to the American Psychological Society for analysis as a basis for future treatment. The stages of reset are; 1) Pride/Vanity, 2) Doubt/Depression, 3) Temptation/Addiction, 4) Guilt/Despair, 5) Fear/Anxiety, 6) Faith/Trust, and 7) Hope/Peace.

The following Seven Stages of Reset will begin with a description, a relevant Bible passage, and a brief commentary.

STAGE 1: PRIDE/VANITY

In *To Dream Again, Again*, Robert Dale says: "I could not imagine what had brought Old First to such an impasse. When I asked a long-time member to explain the situation, he said sadly: 'We could not bring ourselves to change a thing in the old building. After all, it is where Dr. Big Name preached back when he was our pastor in the 1930s and 1940s. 'The ministry of former days under the ministry of a well-known

---

[38] Mayo Clinic Staff, *Job Burnout: How To Spot it And Take Action – Mayo Clinic*, assessed November 2, 2022, https://www.mayoclinic.org/healthy-lifestyles/adult-health/in-debth/burnout/art-20046642.

> pastor paralyzed the Old First congregation. That is nostalgia."[39]

Unlike individual pride, this narrative exemplifies corporate pride in the glory years, which paralyzed a church's congregation and led the city to condemn their historic building. Pride is like cancer in infecting both the congregation and the ministers. It is not just the clergy whose pride leads to a fall; it can sometimes be the vainglory of a congregation. Various levels of pride affect everyone and are a foundation of sin. Yet, this book aims to aid wounded clerics and, indirectly, their congregations.

When churches and pastors fall off their perch, a sequence is initiated. A notable example of uncontrollable pride was the Rev. Jim Bakker, a Pentecostal Holiness preacher, who succumbed to his vanity. He and his wife, Tammy Faye, built an empire filled with an extravagant lifestyle preaching a prosperity gospel, only to see it crumble after a tryst with a church secretary named Jessica Hahn. The damage to the Christian church is incalculable. Every major international news outlet ran headlines, which became a sideshow damaging the church's reputation and shedding a dim light on God.

COMMENTARY ON 1 JOHN 2:15-16

> <u>1 John 2:15-16</u>: Do not love the world or the things in the world. If anyone loves the world, the love of the Father is not in him. For all that is in the world—the desires of the flesh and the desires of the eyes and the pride of life—is not from the Father but is from the world.

Congregations and societies have traditionally placed ministers on a pedestal. This outlook includes anyone who holds a place of authority, such as an elected official, military leader, professor, and

---

[39] Robert D. Dale, *To Dream Again, Again!* (Macon: Nurturing Faith Publishing, 2018), 44.

many other vocations who wield power in commerce, education, and public policy. Pastors need to be reminded that they hold a position of authority and trust because of the God they represent. The irony is that ministers are expected to behave and act with impunity. They are expected to be perfect and avoid mistakes. However, pastors are prone to make mistakes or fail to fulfill promises or expectations. Pastors are subject to sin like everyone else.

Many have fallen to the desires of their hearts and become less effective in their ministry. Pastors must remain constantly vigilant in recognizing that their power is from God. It is God who makes all things possible. Pastors need to remind themselves that they are nothing apart from God.

COMMENTARY ON ROMANS 12:3-8.

> Romans 12: 3-8: Do not conform to the pattern of this world but be transformed by renewing your mind. Then you can test and approve God's will – his good, pleasing, and perfect will. For I say, through the grace given to me, to everyone among you, not to think of himself more highly than he ought to think but to think soberly, as God has dealt to each one a measure of faith. For as we have many members in one goes by, all members do not have the same function, so we, being many, are one body in Christ and individual members of one another.

Clerics should not think more highly of themselves than necessary. A pinch of narcissism and a pound of humility is a recipe for survival in a thankless church. Many churches expect more for less and then wonder why the pastor is not working harder. A pastor is well advised to revisit the limitations of his ministry while renewing his mind. This will transform his church. Paul reminds clerics in this passage that although they live in this world, they are not to conform to the patterns of this world.

This commentary reflects the adoption by many Protestant denominations who have allowed the culture to invade their sanctuaries and erroneously interpret the Holy Scriptures by yielding to the culture rather than the culture bending to the truths of the gospel. It is written in Proverbs 16:18 and transposed into the expression that "pride leads to a fall."[40] Pastors and laity are nothing without God.

Commentary on II Corinthians 10:3-5.

> II Corinthians 10:3-5: Though we walk in the flesh, we do not war according to the flesh. For the weapons of our warfare are not carnal but might in God for pulling down strongholds, casting down arguments on every high thing that exalts itself against the knowledge of God, bringing every thought into captivity to the obedience of Christ and being ready to punish all disobedience when your obedience is fulfilled.

God will cast down every high thing that exalts itself against the knowledge of God. If sin leads the pastor astray, God will reel him back into the fold if his spirit has not been exhausted or become so weary that he cannot continue battling evil forces. Pastors are called to exist apart from the vices of this world. In this consumer-driven society, it is a great temptation to succumb to the desires of this world.

Remaining vigilant to the gospel and disciplined to the Word is the key to a healthy ministry. In many ways, not only is the pastor the example, but he must set the standard that everyone is called to follow. In a sinful world where standards no longer matter, a pastor must remain strong and proclaim the gospel without a waiver. God's Word is the same yesterday, today, and tomorrow.

---

[40] GotQuestions.org. *What does it mean that pride goes before a fall - Proverbs 16:18?*, assessed November 15, 2022, https://www.gotquestions.org/pride-goes-before-a-fall.html.

Commentary on I Corinthians 2:13-16.

I Corinthians 2:13-16: These things we also speak, not in the words which man's wisdom teaches but which the Holy Spirit teaches, comparing spiritual items with spiritual. But the natural man does not receive the things of the Spirit of God, for they are foolishness to him, nor can he know them, because they are spiritually discerned. But he who is spiritual judges all things, yet no one judges him. For who has known the mind of the Lord that he may instruct Him? But we have the mind of Christ.

Brandon Hilgemann says in an article entitled "The One Mistake All Fallen Pastors Make"[41] that pastors who fall in love with the world become more self-righteous and self-serving. They believe that since they are anointed, they are above reproach. They become so ingrained in this world that they have no room for the things of God. Pastors need to remember that they are servants of the Lord. Pastors are called to do God's work on earth and preach the gospel to all nations.

When pastors fall away from God, they become like men who do not understand God's Word. Pastors are expected to lead their congregations like shepherds lead their sheep. They must keep their focus on Calvary's cross. As long as pastors reject the things of this world and stay committed to their work, God will continue to reveal Himself to them and share the wisdom of His word through discernment.

---

[41] Brandon Hilgemann. ProPreacher.com. April 12, 2018, assessed May 10, 2023. https://www.propreacher.com/the-one-mistake-all-preachers-make/

Rev. Dr. Donald R. Hayes, DTh DMin

Commentary on Ezekiel 36:24-27.

> <u>Ezekiel 36:24-27</u>: For I will take you from among the nations, gather you out of all countries, and bring you to your land. Then I will sprinkle clean water on you, and you will be clean; I will cleanse you from all your filthiness and idols. I will give you a new heart and put a new spirit within you; I will take a heart of stone out of your flesh and give you a heart of flesh. I will put My Spirit within you and cause you to walk in My statutes, and you will keep My judgments and do them.

Renewal and restoration begin with recognizing one's fallen nature in the form of pride and vanity coupled with a repentant heart. This turnaround starts with a heart that has warmed to the presence of God. A heart of stone is cold, impenetrable, and unrepentant. God's Word shows that fears, anxieties, and failures constitute a believer who has fallen away from God. Julia Prins Vanderveen says:

> Today's image of a stone has a negative connotation. In Ezekiel's prophecy, God is not pleased with the people's character or behavior. He compares their rebellion to having a heart of stone. So, God sent Ezekiel to speak to the people about changing their ways and reexamining their attitudes and priorities. Yet, before a harsh judgment toward the people, Ezekiel shares this promise that God wants to change their hearts.[42]

Ministers face the same temptations and attractions as everyone else. Broken and wounded clerics need to find wisdom from God's

---

[42] Julia Prins Vanderveen, *A Heart of Stone - Today Daily Devotional*, assessed November 22, 2022, https://todaydevotional.com/devotions/a-heart-of-stone.

Word, which requires an honest evaluation of themselves before meaningful healing begins.

Commentary on Luke 9:46-47.

> Luke 9:46-47: Then a dispute arose among them regarding the most significant. And Jesus, perceiving the thought of their heart, took a little child, set him by him, and said to them, "Whoever receives this little child in my name receives me, and whoever received me receives him who sent me. For he who is least among you will be great."

In Mark 10:25-35, James and John asked Jesus who was the greatest. He answered, "The servant is the greatest." The Sons of Thunder, James and John, harbored an attitude of superiority among their colleagues. This arrogance led to pride in their position and rank, leading them to believe they were set apart for special favors. However, apart from God, this attitude of vainglory entered the hearts and minds of the Apostles and caused division and contempt. Pastors must remain humble and remember that the power in them is from above and not of their own accord. God's Word reveals that the quest for power and superiority often leads to disputes. The church is not immune to clerics vying for power, prestige, or fame. These are among the elixirs that induce people to sin and cause them to fall astray. The hallmark of a righteous pastor is a humble spirit. A prideful pastor has no room for humility. Jesus reminds them in this passage to approach the altar with the mind of a child. They must remember that the least among them is the greatest.

Stage 2: Doubt/Depression

It is not uncommon to feel melancholy, but when doubt and depression last more than a few days and even months, it can be debilitating and devastating to ministers, congregations, and families.

Numerous articles are written on doubt and depression. However, the downward spiral of wounded clergy in this predicament can lead to temptation and addiction. This process underscores the saying, "The bigger they are, the harder they fall." Pastors are well-advised not to think too highly of themselves. They need to make sure they navigate on a solid foundation in the name of Jesus Christ, who calls them according to His purpose.

Yale professor Henri Nouwen says:

> Many ministers, priests, and Christian laity have become disillusioned, bitter, and even hostile when years of hard work bear no fruit and when little change is accomplished. However, building a vocation with expectations of concrete results is like a house on sand instead of solid rock. It even takes away the ability to accept success as a gift."[43] . . ."Many people are convinced that there is something wrong with the world in which they live and feel that cooperation with existing models of living constitutes a kind of betrayal of the self. We see restless and nervous people who cannot concentrate and often suffer from a growing sense of depression.[44]

Pastors often reach a point where they feel their existing models are ineffective. Many feel betrayed by their calling and, in extreme cases, by God. When a pastor reaches this point in his ministry, it is as if he has been cut loose from his anchor and is now adrift in stormy seas.

---

[43] Henri J.M. Nouwen, *The Wounded Healer Ministry in Contemporary Society.* (New York: Random House Publishers, Inc., 1972), 82.

[44] Ibid. Nouwen, *The Wounded Healer Ministry in Contemporary Society*, 38.

Rae Jean Proeschold-Bell and Jason Byassee add to Nouwen's commentary when they say:

> In his book *Man's Search for Meaning*, largely about his experience in Nazi death camps, Frankl concludes that his fellow psychoanalysts are wrong. Human life is not a search for pleasure, as Sigmund Freud premised. It is not based on power, as Alfred Adler, Nietzsche, and others said. Human life is fundamentally a search for meaning. Frankl observed that those who found meaning in their suffering, despite whatever the vile intentions of its inflictors, were those who disproportionately survived. Those who did not find meaning, whose hope gave out, were more quickly among those who died.[45]

Ministers who find themselves burned out and amid doubt and depression are in a vacuum that may need to run the entire course before they hit rock bottom. It is at this point that recovery begins. Attempts are often made along the way yet may be only partially rewarding. A pastor must enter into rescue with a clean slate, not just somewhat clean. When substantial reset and recovery begins, the pride that led to the fall is wholly exorcised from them.

COMMENTARY ON MATTHEW 11:1-6.

> Matthew 11:1-6: Now it came to pass when Jesus had finished instructing his twelve disciples, he went on to teach and preach in Galilee. And when John had heard in prison about the works of Christ, he sent two of his disciples to ask him, "Are you the one who is to come, or should we

---

[45] Rae Jean Proeschold-Bell and Jason Byassee, *Faithful and Fractured - Responding to the Clergy Health Crisis* (Grand Rapids: Baker Academic, 2018), 44.

expect another?" Jesus answered and said to them, "Go and tell John the things which you hear and see: The blind see and the awkward walk; the lepers are cleansed and the deaf hear; the dead are raised, and the poor have the gospel preached to them. And blessed is he who is not offended because of Me."

If a pastor ever doubts Jesus, he is like John the Baptist. In Matthew 11:11, Jesus said: "Truly, I tell you, among those born of women, there has not risen anyone greater than John the Baptist, yet whoever is least in the kingdom of heaven is greater than he." Nevertheless, John the Baptist asked his disciples to discover if Jesus was the true Messiah. This is evidence of doubt and depression. It caused John the Baptist to wonder whether Yeshua[46] was the Messiah. Many clerics and laity struggle with doubt and depression.

It is reported that Rev. Dwight L. Moody suffered greatly from depression. He said, "I have struggled with anxiety and depression for 15 years and have always tried to manage it independently. I grew up in a Christian home and the church, but I never knew how to come before God and ask him for help humbly."[47] Doubt and depression are not the traits congregations expect of clergies. Doubt, created by God, is helpful when it leads ministers to discern the truth. Doubt and depression can become a stumbling block for wounded clergies, leading them away from their ministries.

---

[46] Doug Hershey. *Yeshua: The Meaning of the Hebrew Name of Jesus – FIRM Israel*, assessed December 10, 2022, https://firmisrael.org/learn/who-is-yeshua-meaning-of-hebrew-namejesus/#.~text+The%20Meaning%20of%20Jesus%20Hebrew%20Name%20Yeshua&text=This%20unique%20name%20of%20God,the%20most%20significant)%20means%20salvation.

[47] Maggie Hubbard. The D.L. Moody Center. Anxiety, Depression, And The Christian Life. Accessed May 12, 2023, https://moodycenter.org > articles.

The Battlefield of Faith

Commentary on James 4:1-5.

> James 4:1-5: Where do wars and fights come from among you? Do they not come from your desires for pleasure that war in your members? You lust and do not have. You murder and covet and cannot obtain. You fight a war. Yet you do not have because you do not ask. You ask and do not receive because you ask amiss, that you may spend it on your pleasures. You adulterous people, don't you know that friendship with the world is enmity with God? Whoever, therefore, wants to be a friend of the world makes himself an enemy of God. Or do you think the Scripture says in vain, "The Spirit who dwells in us yearns jealously?"

Where do fights and wars begin? God's Word says they come from the devices and desires of our hearts. When clerics fall away from the source of their calling, the lines between heavenly things and worldly things become blurred. Ministers can become so far removed from God that they adopt the world's ways and ignore the ways of heaven. Their actions, prejudices, desires, and opinions become their dialogue rather than the tenets of God. It is a stage where the pastor can repent and return to God or remain separated from God forever. Scripture alludes to this character or condition as being adulterous. An adulterer betrays his mate. He leaves the comfort and security of his home to seek the ways of this world. It is a dead-end street. Scripture also says it leads to destruction. No good can come from God to a preacher who has committed adultery in his heart. If he repents, he will regain favor with God, who will hear his pleas and answer his prayers. Until such time, he will live apart from God in misery, wondering why.

Commentary on Luke 5:16.

<u>Luke 5:16:</u> So, he often withdrew into the wilderness and prayed.

Jesus escaped from the labors of his ministry and landed in the wilderness to pray and meditate with his Father. This helped him to regain his strength. This passage clearly shows the necessity for a retreat at regular intervals for pastors to pray and meditate so they can reconnect with their calling. Jesus would withdraw to these places of respite that the Bible calls a wilderness. It may only be a hill or ravine, but the essence is that He was alone with God. Nevertheless, it was a secure place away from the hustle and bustle of the maddening crowds and the demanding disciples. Jesus poured so much of himself into his ministry that it left him needing a reset to reclaim his energy. Pastors have the exact needs of respite as Jesus. They need a quiet place to reconnect with their thoughts as Jesus was ministered to by heavenly angels and his father. Jesus would pray and meditate and may have raised his voice in a song like King David. He used his time in the wilderness to recharge his spirit and reembark into the fray.

Stage 3: Temptation/Addiction

After leaving pride and vanity in stage one and doubt and depression in stage two clearly in their wake, ministers enter stage three. They have entered a weakened state where temptation and addiction abound. In this stage, all sorts of calamities can occur. No one knows what goes through the mind of a pastor who has fallen to stage three. Every case is unique, and he may find himself between a rock and a hard place.

What we do know is that many have reported turning to addictive drugs or alcohol for a source of relief. Perry Noble, the founding pastor of New Spring Church, is one such pastor who fell from grace with the church. Media outlets reported that alcohol was a contributing factor in his decline. Cloistered in a pastor's mind is a lingering voice that becomes a constant companion suggesting all the wrong prescriptions to relieve the pain from the suffering. This is a critical juncture for the wounded clergy, and how it is treated can lengthen or lessen the time in recovery.

> McIntosh and Rima say: Even when the basic assumptions are acknowledged to some degree, many in the Christian community relegate the problem entirely to spiritual warfare and demonic attack. Fallen spiritual leaders are often considered casualties in a cosmic spiritual battle and little else. But the problem is not easily dismissed. With the baby boomer generation's emergence and its members' ascendence to leadership positions during the 1970s and 1980s, America and the church discovered a generation plagued by a plethora of personal dysfunctions. Whether it was the dysfunction of co-dependence, addictive behaviors, obsessive-compulsive disorders, narcissistic personality disorder, adult children of alcoholics (ACOA), or any of a host of others, personal dysfunctions became a badge of the boomer generation and a focal point of church ministries.[48]

Temptations that lead to addictions are considered the most troubling stage in the seven-stage reset because they are challenging to treat. While stages two through five are the major battles, none scars a pastor like stage three. Pastors carry these wounds for the length of their ministries. Pastors should take solace in knowing that Jesus was pierced and scarred from His battles with the dangers and enemies of His kingdom. While the scars may not be physical, emotional scars

---

[48] McIntosh and Rima, *Overcoming the Dark Side of Leadership*, 15.

are just as painful and long-lasting without proper treatment and care. Pastors must remember that "By His stripes, we are healed."[49]

COMMENTARY ON EPHESIANS 4:2-24.

> Ephesians 4:20-24: But you have not so learned Christ, if indeed you have heard Him and have been taught by Him, as the truth is in Jesus: that you were put off, concerning your former conduct, the older adult who grows corrupt according to the deceitful lusts, and be renewed in the spirit of your mind, and that you put on the new man, which was created according to God, in true righteousness and holiness.

The weight of temptations can be overwhelming. If unaddressed, they can lead to addictions, and this leads to destruction. Pastors wonder, "Is God not omnipotent? Omnipresent? Omniscient?" If God is all these things, and he calls me, why did this happen to me? Indeed, God is all these things. He experienced all the challenges pastors face because He was a complete man and God. The truth is in Jesus. If a pastor cannot let go of his past, God says, "Therefore, if any man is in Christ, he is a new creature: old things are passed away; behold, all things have become new."[50] Again, in Isaiah 43, we read: "Forget the former things; do not dwell on the past. See, I am doing a new thing! Now it springs up: do you not perceive it? I am making a way in the desert and streams in the wasteland."[51]

A pastor once tried to counsel a parishioner who said he had many "pet peeves." He suggested that the man discard them but was met with an unkind gesture. It became clear that the man had no desire to let go of his pets. Since he had been with them so long, he felt he would not be alone without them. Not letting go of the past

---

[49] Isa. 53:5.
[50] 2 Cor. 5:17.
[51] Isa. 43:18-19.

can lead to a bitter end. In Luke, we read, "But Jesus said to him, 'No one, after putting his hand to the plow and looking back, is fit for the kingdom of God.'"[52] Many pastors face the same dilemma as this parishioner. Letting go of the past takes effort.

Commentary on James 4:7-10.

> <u>James 4:7-10</u>: Therefore, submit to God. Resist the devil, and he will flee from you. Draw near to God, and he will draw near to you. Cleanse your hands, you sinners; purify your hearts; you double-minded. Lament and mourn and weep! Let your laughter be turned to mourning and your joy to gloom. Humble yourselves in the sight of the Lord, and He will lift you.

The Bible tells us that the source of evil is the devil. Pastors are reminded that when they fall into temptation, they must resist the devil and flee as Joseph did with Potiphar's wife, even when they risk imprisonment. Addictions manifest in many forms, including sex, drugs, and alcohol, which is encouraged in the Rock and Roll nomenclature. Habits often led to denial, and this bespeaks a spirit of being double-minded. Here pastors are being reminded that they cannot have their cake and eat it too. They must decide between good and evil. They must choose between living for the devil or living for God. They must decide between the world and heaven. Their eternal destiny is linked to their decisions. When a victim of addiction admits his defeat, he is at the repentance stage. Here he can face his demons and begin renewing his relationship with God. His heart will become pure as he submits to God, who will elevate him.

---

[52] Luke 9:62.

Commentary on Matthew 6:9-13.

> Matthew 6:9-13: Therefore, do not be like them. For your Father knows the things you need before you ask Him. In this manner, therefore, pray: Our Father in heaven, hallowed be your name, your kingdom come, your will be done, on earth as it is in heaven. Give us today our daily bread. And forgive us our debts, as we also have forgiven our debtors. And lead us not into temptation but deliver us from the evil one.

The final admonishment in the Lord's Prayer underscores the importance of being aware of evil. It directs clergy to focus on the presence of sin and its destructive nature upon all people.

Pastors should remember that God already knows their needs and, as a loving Father, desires to bring His children peace and joy.

Commentary on I Corinthians 10:13.

> I Corinthians 10:11-13: These things happened to them as examples and were written down as warnings for us, on whom the culmination of the ages has come. So, if you think you are standing firm, be careful not to fall! No temptation has overtaken you except what is common to humankind. And God is faithful: he will not let you be tempted beyond what you can bear. But when you are tempted, He will make a way out so that you can endure it.

There is no sin that God cannot forgive save the rejection of his Son Jesus. Temptation is universal, and there are no new temptations under the sun. Everyone, including pastors, has been subject to temptation. How pastors survive temptation is a work in progress as pastors serve the church. God will not allow temptation beyond the limits of each person. God provides an escape when temptation arises. Jesus was tempted throughout his ministry. In each case, evidence shows he confronted temptation by quoting Scripture. Calling upon Jesus' name amid temptation is a skill that needs to be honed into a habit. The word of the street is that ministers are tempted more because they are the frontline troops fighting against evil. If sin can destroy a minister, then nothing can stop evil from running rampant against their congregations with no shepherd to protect them.

Commentary on Galatians 6:1-3.

> Galatians 6:1-3: Brothers and sisters, if anyone is caught in a sin, you who live by the Spirit should restore that person gently. But watch yourselves, or you may also be tempted. Carry each other's burdens; this way, you will fulfill the law of Christ. If anyone thinks they are something when they are not, they deceive themselves. Each one should test their actions. Then they can take pride in themselves alone, without comparing themselves to someone else, for each one should carry their load. Nevertheless, the one who receives instruction in the world should share all good things with their instructor.

When sin engulfs a pastor, he must repent and ask forgiveness from God. Then God will, as a good pastor, gently admonish the sinner to repent as instructed. However, once cleansed, he must be careful not to be a repeat offender. Pastors should journey in each other's burdens. It is easy for a pastor to fall into an elevated sense of superiority. This is easy to do, but every coin has two sides. God created all things, and Satan has turned around the meaning and purpose for all things good. For example, hating sin is good, but hating someone is not. Living righteously is good, but self-righteous behavior is not. Pride in one's accomplishment is good but using it as a wedge to demean or harm another is not good.

The world teaches us to "Be your master...control your destiny . . . you are the greatest." These are the monikers of today. Frank Sinatra[53] popularized a song entitled "I Did It My Way," which spent seventy-five weeks on the United Kingdom's Top 40. If a person succumbs to the world, the world will be his reward. However, ministers should avoid this temptation, yet many have fallen victim to the world. Pastors are expected to do things God's way, not the way of evil. All believers are encouraged to store their treasures in heaven, not this world.

STAGE 4: GUILT/DESPAIR

Guilt and grief are nearly synonymous. Therefore, to address accountability, an examination of suffering is worth noting. In *Helping Those in Grief – What to Say and What Not to Say: A Guide to Help You Care for Others*, H. Norman Wright says:

> Weathering Life's Storms, on the coast, residents must prepare when they get a storm warning. They must secure lawn furniture or any items that could blow around and injure them. They must anchor down boats and strap them to something more secure, like the pier. The fierce winds may come, but anchored and securely tied to the strong pier, the boat is still there. This is like our hope during stormy times of grief. It would be best to remain anchored to those people or beliefs who may be a source of strength at that time. God often chooses to minister to us through other people or His Word. If we do not anchor with the right resources, we will be blown apart when the storms hit.[54]

---

[53] Kitty Kelley, *His Way: An Unauthorized Biography of Frank Sinatra* (New York: Random House Publishing, Inc., 2015), 89.

[54] H. Norman Wright, *Helping Those in Grief: What to Say and What Not to Say. A Guide to Help You Care for Others,* (Ventura: Regal from Gospel Light, 2010), 205.

The Battlefield of Faith

According to an article in *Psychology Today* by Jonice Webb[55], guilt is the breeding ground of grief. Often, when the wounded clergy exits out of addictions into a better place, it is accompanied by a feeling of "guilty grief." We usually do not describe grief in situations other than the death or loss of a loved one. The similarity is that we find ourselves grieving and thus feeling guilty about our fall from grace. This is not a pity party; instead, it is coming to terms with the effects of bad choices, self-righteous behavior, or in many cases, situations beyond the control of the afflicted.

Following stage three of temptation and addiction, the wounded pastor falls into an abyss of guilt and disappointment from a failed ministry, leading to despair. Paraplegic Joni Tada shares her thoughts with Steven Estes in their book *When God Weeps*. They say:

> Who can endure such emptiness? I am reminded of this whenever I see the famous The Scream, a painting by Norwegian artist Edvard Munch. It is a horrific portrayal of despair, a painting of a gaunt and ghoulish figure, twisted and tormented, with eyes wide and mouth open. The figure is wailing, and horror is magnified because you cannot hear its cry. He is a painted figure, and he is a silent scream. A pure and distilled scream of despair.[56]

The popularity of this painting shows how humanity connects to this depiction of despair. This example is not lost on clergy who give up and leave their pulpits in record numbers.

---

[55] Jonice Webb, Why Grief is a Breeding Ground for Guilt, *Psychology Today*, accessed November 30, 2022. https://www.psychologytoday.com/s/blog/childhood-emotional-neglect/202210/why-grief-is-breeding-ground-guilt.

[56] Joni Eareckson Tada and Steven Estes, *When God Weeps* (Grand Rapids: Zondervan, 1997), 152.

Rev. Dr. Donald R. Hayes, DTh DMin

Commentary on Colossians 1:9-14.

> <u>Colossians 1:9-14</u>: Since we heard about you, we have not stopped praying for you. We continually ask God to fill you with the knowledge of his will through all the wisdom and understanding that the Spirit gives so that you may live a life worthy of the Lord and please him in every way: bearing fruit in every good work, growing in the knowledge of God, being strengthened with all power according to his glorious might so that you may have great endurance and patience, and giving joyful thanks to the Father, who has qualified you to share in the inheritance of his holy people in the kingdom of light. He has rescued us from the dominion of darkness and brought us into the realm of the Son he loves, in whom we have redemption and forgiveness.

Ministers need not feel guilt or despair, which fosters anxiety and fear. Paul reminds the Colossians that God has delivered his people from the powers of darkness. The same God releases clerics from the grip of guilt and despair, which lives in the dominion of darkness. In his miraculous ways, God has transferred his believers into the kingdom of light of his beloved Son. Pastors and congregations are heirs to the kingdom. If heirs, then they are also sons of the God most high. Clerics should continue to pray for each other to undergird and prepare them for future battles. They will experience sheer joy from the victories while suffering tremendous guilt and despair from the losses or failures.

There are many hills and valleys along the journey of ministers. In many ways, the pilgrimage is lonely and tiresome. Many followers with noble intentions attempt but fail to share the burdens of pastors. However, everyone knows the responsibility of discipleship. Many pastors experience high personal and professional costs.

Twentieth-century martyr Deitrick Bonhoeffer described this cost as cheap grace versus costly grace. If the pastor recovers to reclaim his calling, he must find that "The Christian must achieve renunciation, to practice self-effacement, to distinguish his life from the life of the world."[57] The late Bishop of Chichester, the Rt. Rev. G.K.A. Bell wrote in his forward that Bonhoeffer had said, "When Christ calls a man, he bids him come and die."[58] Christ counterweighs this message with hope and peace.

COMMENTARY ON JOHN 15:18-21.

> John 15:18-21: If the world hates you, remember that the world hated me first. If you belong to the world, it will love you as its own. As it is, you do not belong to the world, but I have chosen you out of the world. That is why the world hates you. Remember what I told you, a servant is not greater than his master. If they persecuted me, they would crush you also. If they obeyed my teaching, they would abide by yours also. They will treat you because of my name, for they do not know the one who sent me.

Some pastors will face a breakdown due to burnout or job-related stress. This passage predicts that the world will persecute any clergy or laity who choose to follow Christ. The world will chastise the pastor who makes Jesus the Lord of his life. One reason the world will hate pastors is that they are called to proclaim a different worldview. Christians are called to live by a set of standards when the world has no meaningful guidelines.

The world is chaotic and confused, while the people of God are taught to practice order and clarity in their lives. Believers are found in good company because Jesus was hated and persecuted

---

[57] Dietrich Bonhoeffer, *The Cost of Discipleship* (New York: Simon & Schuster), 44.
[58] Bonhoeffer, *The Cost of Discipleship*, Forward.

before we were, and we will be blessed for enduring the persecution. Opposition to pastors will be inevitable. Pastors should not enter the ministry from a position of naivety and harbor no illusions of a perfect life. The more a pastor proclaims the gospel, the more he will be ostracized, segregated, rejected, and alienated.

Commentary on I Timothy 1:15-16.

> I Timothy 1:15-16: Here is a trustworthy saying that deserves full acceptance: Christ Jesus came into the world to save sinners, of whom I am the worst. But for that very reason, I was shown mercy so that in me, the worst of sinners, Christ Jesus might display His immense patience as an example for those who would believe in Him and receive eternal life.

God created man in His image.[59] Like Paul, who wrote this letter to Timothy, are faithful pastors with the same hopes, dreams, desires, and faults as anyone. Yet, they are the agents of God doing his bidding on earth. These faithful ministers fall in the order of Melchizedek.[60] Since humanity fell from grace through Adam, God sent his Son into the world to save sinners. In his humility, Paul admitted that he was chief among sinners. Paul displayed a humble and contrite spirit. He lived with a servant's heart, just like Jesus, humanity's only hope for salvation. All are sinners except by the grace of God through His son Jesus Christ. Pastors are servants of God to emulate His humility and exemplify the light that emanates through Jesus to brighten this dark world.

---

[59] Gen. 1:27.
[60] Moses Y. Lee, *Who Is Melchizedek?* accessed December 20, 2022, https://www.thegospelcoalition.org/article/jesus-Melchizedek.

The Battlefield of Faith

COMMENTARY ON GENESIS 2:1-3.

> <u>Genesis 2:1-3</u>: Thus, the heavens and earth, and all the most of them, were finished. And on the seventh day, God ended His work which He had done, and He rested on the seventh day from all His work which He had done. Then God blessed the seventh day and sanctified it because He rested from all His work which God had created and made.

Pastors report they work too many hours without rest. They feel guilty when the needs of their church members never cease to end. Saying "no" to a church member, even when it is in the best interest of the pastor, has been the straw that broke the camel's back in many a wounded pastor. Even God rested from his labors on the seventh day, as indicated in the book of Genesis. Most clerics are self-employed, so adhering to a strict schedule is nearly impossible. Clerics work or are on-call 24/7, meaning their bodies and minds become weary after years of laboring in the fields without proper rest. In the Pastoral Care, Inc. Survey, seventy-eight percent of pastors report that rest, vacation time, or respite time is missing from their schedule.

One of the main objectives of Slains Ministries will be to help clerics find balance in their lives and discover ways to keep a schedule that provides for rest. The challenge for clerics is that no one knows when a death or a hospital need or crisis occurs, which requires the services of pastors. This is the paradox of the calling. Ironically, many people see clerics as having too much time to themselves. Thus, many church members do not recognize the hours of labor and preparation for services, not including preparation for sermons behind the scenes. Clerics of all denominations are full-time in every way, for which many are not adequately compensated. Pastoral Care,

Inc.[61] reports that fifty-seven percent do not believe they receive a living wage. This is one of the leading indexes that cause pastors to leave their ministries.

Stage 5: Fear/Anxiety

Transitioning from stage four, one awakens to the unsettling conditions of anxiety and fear. This stage can cause wounded clergy to become frozen and unable to cope with their daily responsibilities. This can become an extension of depression in which symptoms include the inability to function. Anxiety can be debilitating because it forces a man to look at his greatest fear, death. It can cause psychosomatic problems that affect the body through elevated blood pressure, leading to cardiovascular conditions and strokes.

According to The Indigo Project, the greatest fear is death.[62] It is "The mother of all fears – and, as some theorists suggest, the only true reason we fear anything at all." There are five responses to fear: fight, flight, freeze, flop, and friend.[63] And some would add a sixth response: fawn. I found in a quotation, "Fear is the path to the Dark Side. Fear leads to anger; anger leads to hate; hate leads to suffering."[64]

Tada and Estes address the transition of anxiety and fear into anger where in *When God Weeps,* they say:

> Anger has a dark side too. It has incredible potential to destroy. It digresses into black energy that demands immediate release and relief. It despises being vulnerable and helpless. It relishes

---

[61] Pastoral Care, Inc., *Statistics for Pastors,* accessed December 15, 2022, https://www.pastoralcareinc.com/statistics.

[62] Our Four Greatest Fears (And What They Say About Us), accessed April 14, 2023, https://www.theindigoproject.com.

[63] The 5 F's: fight, flight, freeze, flop, and friend – Rape Crisis, accessed April 14, 2023, https://rapecrisis.org.UK > get-help.

[64] 17 Inspiring Quotes to Help You Face Your Fears | Inc., accessed March 14, 2023, https://www.inc.com > Sims-Wyeth.

staying in control. It loathes dependence on God and gains macabre pleasure in spreading the poison of mistrust. Ironically, this sort of anger . . . unrighteous anger—turns on us. It is a liar, offering us satisfaction when in truth, it guts us and leaves us empty while unrighteous anger—anger that leads us away from God—sucks our hearts' last vestige of hope. We stop caring, stop feeling. We commit a silent suicide of the soul, and sullen despair moves in like a terrible damp fog, deadening our hearts to the hope that we will ever be rescued, redeemed, and happy again.[65]

Ironically, anger leads us away from God. Then, we are prone to adopt a fit of righteous anger that takes away our last lifeline to God: hope.

Commentary on Joshua 1:8-9.

Joshua: 1:8-9: This Book of the Law shall not depart from your mouth, but you shall meditate in it day and night, that you may observe according to all that is written in it. For then, you will make your way prosperous, and then you will have success. Have I not commanded you? Be strong and courageous. Do not be afraid; do not be discouraged, for the Lord your God will be with you wherever you go.

God commands us not to be afraid or discouraged. He says with authority that He will be with us wherever we go. This short passage of Scripture should strengthen the ministers of the gospel. God recognized that ministers are targets in this world. Evil wants

---

[65] Tada and Estes, *When God Weeps*, 152.

to silence the message of hope, peace, and joy. Ultimately, the world wants to bury the Good News so it will never be spoken again. Jesus is the world's hope, the source of peace, and the joy of our salvation.

We are the defenders of the Word of God. We are commanded not to be afraid. Fear is self-defeating. We already know who wins the ultimate battle. God has equipped clerics to battle evil, but we quickly become weakened by the sheer magnitude of the battlefield. Joshua knew this quite well as he led the Israelites into the Promised Land of Milk and Honey.[66]

Commentary on Mark 4:34-39.

> <u>Mark 4:34-39</u>: On that day, when evening had come, he said to them, "Let us go across to the other side." And leaving the crowd behind, they took him in the boat just as he was. Other boats were with him. A great windstorm arose, and the waves beat into the boat so that the boat was already swamped. But he was in the stern asleep on the cushion, and they woke him up and said to him, "Teacher, do you not care that we are perishing?' He woke up, rebuked the wind, and said to the sea, "Peace, be still!"[67] Then the wind ceased, and there was a dead calm.

Kirk Byron Jones writes in *Rest in the Storm* about his bouts with stress. He says that despite the clerics' best intentions, sometimes things go off track. The trip can become life-threatening, like the disciples who launched from shore for a peaceful eight-mile journey across Galilee to Decapolis. Jones writes about calming the storm inside. He says, "This Scripture touched me deeply. Suddenly, in my mind, I was the one on a boat in a raging storm. For the past few weeks, I had been caught in the storm of my life. Never had I felt so

---

[66] Exod. 3:8.
[67] Mark 4:35-39.

vulnerable and unable to control what was going on in my mind and body."[68]

He adds how this passage was a gift of healing when, over the years, it had been a source of encouragement when facing fearful conditions. He says: "I am convinced that both what happened and what did not happen on the boat that night offer critical insights into resisting overload and overdrive in everyday living. If we can understand and practice the behaviors Jesus exhibited on the boat, we can experience peace amid the storms of life-threatening stress."[69] Finding peace that passes all understanding, as Jones did, is a critical step in this stage of the seven-part journey. The sooner a pastor reaches this emotional and spiritual development, the sooner his recovery begins.

COMMENTARY ON PSALM 23:1-6.

> Psalm 23:1-6: The Lord is my Shepherd; I shall not want. He made me lie down in green pastures; he leadeth me beside the still waters. He restoreth my soul; he leadeth me in the paths of righteousness for His name's sake. Yea, though I walk through the valley of the shadow of death, I will fear no evil; for thou art with me; thy rod and thy staff comfort me. Thou preparest a table before me in the presence of my enemies; thou anointest my head with oil; my cup runneth over. Surely goodness and mercy shall follow me all the days of my life, and I will dwell in the house of the Lord forever.

This passage is one of the most recognized in the Old Testament. It is the one that is often memorized. Children love to read it because it comforts them, knowing that the "Lord is my Shepherd" is there

---

[68] Kirk Byron Jones, *Rest in The Storm* (Valley Forge: Judson Press, 2021), 23.
[69] Jones, *Rest in The Storm*. 24.

to protect and provide for them. Next, "I walk through the valley of the Shadow of Death" refers to evil and death. This is the path pastors must navigate because it is through this valley where all the landmines are located, unlike the mountain trail above the fray of life.

A pastor lives in this world's highways, byways, and gutters. The shadow of death is all around. Evil is stalking everyone, primarily clergy, on the frontlines of the war of good versus evil. This passage comforts clergy because it holds their enemies at bay while preparing a place of refreshment at the table of life. Clergy are reminded that they are anointed, and their cups will run over with abundance in the joys of serving the Lord.

Stage 6: Faith/Trust

The author of Proverbs says, "Trust in the Lord with all your heart and lean not on your understanding; in all your ways acknowledge him, and he will make your paths straight."[70] This sixth stage is identified as the safety net. The worst of the stages are behind when pastors arrive at this juncture. The story of faith and trust is found in the holocaust, which has been studied and debated for nearly eighty years. The question on most people's minds is, "How can a loving God allow such atrocities?" Nobel Prize recipient and Holocaust survivor Elie Wiesel spent his life keeping the memories of this human tragedy in people's minds. His purpose was never to let this happen again.

However, today, we still see man's inhumanity to man. It seems that humanity fails to learn its lessons. The horror of the holocaust underscores the tragedy of the cross where Christ was crucified. As Wiesel stated, "Where was God in all of this?"[71] There are many similarities, especially the death of innocent parties.

Wiesel helped inform the world that despite the deaths of innocent victims, there was a view of God's mercy. It came as hope,

---

[70] Prov. 3:5-6.
[71] Elie Wiesel, *Night* (New York: Hill and Wang, 2017), 143.

which led to a renewed faith in God. Life is far from perfect and filled with risk. However, life without risk, without trials and tribulations, is not fulfilling. From tragedy and suffering springs forth faith and, ultimately, trust in God.

When pastors fall from their pride and vainglory, they go through the valley of the shadow of death. In this dark and troubled time, they discover who God is and either become restored or fall into oblivion. Humanity seeks God when times are bad, not always good. This is likely by God's design. God wants a relationship with his creation, and pastors need a relationship with God.

> Elie Wiesel says: A Jew defines himself more by what troubles him than what reassures him. Jewish or not, morally concerned and vitally religious persons can be defined similarly. Griffin (David Ray) worries that time and energy spent protesting God would be better spent 'echoing the divine call.' His assessment of my (John R. Roth) outlook overemphasizes blame, but a protesting antitheodicy (vindication of God) emphasizes responsibility—God's and humanity's. The purpose of this emphasis is not to dwell on blame but lucidly to take stock of our situation in the world. Here the tradition of process theology is simply different from the one that informs a protesting antitheodicy. Through its distinctive form of protest, the latter underscores the divine call. Religious vitality depends on more than one way of encountering the divine.[72]

Thus, encountering the divine is where a pastor's faith is renewed, rebuilding his trust in God and each other. When pastors fall from grace, God beckons them back to Him. Often, pastors must

---

[72] Stephen T. Davis, Ed., *Encountering Evil: Live Options in Theodicy, A New Edition*, (Louisville: Westminster John Knox Press, 2001), 35.

endure hardships, and through the lessons learned, they find purpose and meaning in their lives.

Commentary on Romans 12:6-8

> Romans 12:6-8: Having then gifts differing according to the grace that is given to us, let us use them: if prophecy, let us prophesy in proportion to our faith; of ministry, let us use it in our ministering; he who teaches, in teaching: he who exhorts, in the exhortation he who gives, with liberality: let who leads, with diligence: he who shows mercy, with cheerfulness.

When clerics enter this stage of faith and trust, having left behind the grip of fear and anxiety, they are well on their way to recovery. Found in that realm are gifts granted according to the proportion of their faith. When a pastor reaches this point in the seven stages, his wounds have been addressed, and he is on the way to renewal. He has weathered the storm and wakes each day with a purpose.

> Tim Clinton and Joshua Straub say: When we feel out of control, we don't have to give up in despair. God will use every struggle, heartache, and moment of confusion to teach us life's most important lessons. In his letter to the Christians in Rome, Paul explained this point. Paul concluded that suffering is God's classroom. He wrote: We also rejoice in our sufferings because we know that suffering produces perseverance; perseverance, character; and character, hope. It does not disappoint us because God has poured

his love into our hearts by the Holy Spirit, whom he has given us (Romans 5:3-5).[73]

The pastor has plugged into God, his teacher, and reset his calling to become a productive minister again. Those gifts are the strength of a renewed ministry, including the skills of teaching and exhortation of preaching, receiving the advantages of the spirit leading to joy and tender mercies. These are the gifts for completing the seven stages of reset.

Commentary on II Thessalonians 3:1-5.

> II Thessalonians 3:1-5: Finally, brethren, pray for us, that the word of the Lord may run swiftly and be glorified, just as it is with you, and that we may be delivered from unreasonable and wicked men; for not all have faith. But the Lord is faithful, who will establish you and guard you from the evil one. And we have confidence in the Lord concerning you, that you do and will do what we command you. Now may the Lord direct your hearts into God's love and the patience of Christ.

The Bible reminds pastors that not every church member is faithful so that the church pews may be full of enemies of the gospel. This has happened more than clerics have hoped or imagined in their ministries. Over the decades, there have been untold accounts of parishioners or laity who have verbally attacked their pastors and dismissed them from their positions, many without cause. Most attacks were not physical, but character assassination and gaslighting happen more than we know.

---

[73] Tim Clinton and Joshua Straub. *God Attachment: When You Believe, Act, And Feel the Way You Do About God* (New York: Simon & Shuster, Inc., 2010), 219.

Dennis R. Maynard says that according to the research of Gene Wood, author of *Leading Turnaround Churches*, "Thirteen hundred Christian pastors are forced to resign their parishes every month! They are forced to do so without cause and often under a cloud of rumor and insinuation that will haunt them for the rest of their ministry. Another twelve hundred leave their ministry monthly, citing stress, church-related issues, family issues, or burnout." [74]

COMMENTARY ON I PETER 5:6-9.

> <u>I Peter 5:6-9</u>: Therefore, humble yourselves under the mighty hand of God that He may exalt you in due time, casting all your care upon Him, for He cares for you. Be sober and vigilant because your adversary, the devil, walks around like a roaring lion, seeking whom he may devour. Resist him, steadfast in the faith, knowing that the same sufferings are experienced by your brotherhood in the world.

Pastors are certainly in the devil's crosshairs since they are the shepherds called to lead and protect God's flocks. On the battlefield, military chaplains are provided with a bodyguard since they cannot carry a weapon under the rules of the Geneva Convention. And for their enemy, a premium is placed on the chaplain's head for their bounty. The theory is that if the spiritual leader is cut off, troops will lose the will to fight. Pastors are no different in civilian life, except their battlefield is a spiritual warzone. They are not immune to the evil that roams the earth to devour anyone or anything in its path.

A pastor must come to terms with how he arrived at his crossroads. If mistakes were made, then he must learn from them. He must look for ways to minimize the errors, remove them, and replace them with positive results. A pastor battles for the hearts, minds,

---

[74] Dennis R. Maynard, *When Sheep Attack!* (USA: BookSurge Publishers, 2010), 10.

and souls of the lost and, in turn, the faithful. This requires him to be vigilant because evil stalks the children of the light in this dark world.[75] Evil is often overlooked or diluted in the minds of many worldwide, while the devil is the danger lurking in our midst.

Commentary on Matthew 5:1-2;10-12.

> Matthew 5: 11-12: And seeing the multitudes, He went up on a mountain, and when He was seated, His disciples came to Him. Then He opened His mouth and taught them, saying: . . . Blessed are those who are persecuted for righteousness's sake, for theirs is the kingdom of heaven. Blessed are you when they revile and persecute you and falsely say all kinds of evil against you for My sake. Rejoice and be exceedingly glad; for great is your reward in heaven, for they persecuted the prophets before you.

In his Sermon on the Mount, Jesus offers comforting words to his followers, especially his disciples, who were called to shepherd his flock. Ultimately, these are words of comfort for the wounded spiritual warrior. No one likes war, but individuals are forced to engage the enemy of God, whether as warriors or as a support community. The battle of good versus evil has been waging as far back as Eden and has ebbed and flowed over the centuries. Although wars are never pleasant, they must be engaged for the living to become the righteous servants God has called them to be.

Jesus' commandments prepare the minister for the inevitable. If a pastor proclaims the gospel, he will be persecuted. When pastors are oppressed, Jesus tells them to rejoice and be glad, for if they persecuted Me, they would persecute you. A reward will be great in heaven because they are counted with the prophets and saints—

---

[75] Eph. 5:7-14.

hopefully, many pastors who suffer do so not for the prize but to fulfill their calling.

Commentary on Ephesians 4:1-7.

> Ephesians 4:1-7: As a prisoner for the Lord, I urge you to live a life worthy of the calling you have received. Be completely humble and gentle; be patient, bearing one another in love. Make every effort to keep the unity of the Spirit through the bond of peace. There is one body and one Spirit, just as you were called to one hope when you were called; one Lord, one faith, one baptism, one God and Father of all, who is over all and through all and in all.

Pastors, preachers, priests, bishops, overseers, deacons, and elders are all members of one Lord, one faith, one baptism, and one God. Every spiritual leader from all Christian denominations is welcomed at Slains Ministries. This ministry of healing and reset will not distinguish between Protestant denominations and Catholics. This principle adheres to the tenet of unity in Christ Jesus. The more believers practice the principles of their faith, the issues that divide denominations and Christianity will no longer be divisive. Notably, a common enemy wants to devour the Church, which is not a different denomination. This common enemy is evil. This fact promotes a life worthy of their calling and produces one body and one Spirit.

Commentary on Ephesians 6:10-13.

> Ephesians 6:10-13: Finally, my brethren, be strong in the Lord and the power of His might. Put on the whole armor of God so that you can stand against the devil's wiles. For we do not wrestle against flesh and blood, but against principalities, against powers, against the rulers

of the darkness of this age, against spiritual hosts of wickedness in the heavenly places. Therefore, take up the whole armor of God, that you may be able to withstand the evil day, and having done all, to stand.

Clerics are spiritual warriors. They resemble military warriors who wage war against tyranny worldwide. The difference is that military warriors fight against flesh and blood, while spiritual warriors fight against evil that is out to kill souls. Spiritual warfare is like any military battle where the fighting is fierce. Spiritual warriors need time to step aside and recharge their hearts and minds for the fight to reclaim the souls of the lost and lonely, the downtrodden and neglected, and the abused and abandoned. Spiritual and military warriors face similar obstacles in their respective missions. Many face post-traumatic challenges that develop into disorders that require psychological and medical help and treatment.

COMMENTARY ON EPHESIANS 6:14-17.

Ephesians 6:14-17: Stand firm then, with the belt of truth buckled around your waist, with the breastplate of righteousness in place, and with your feet fitted with the readiness that comes from the gospel of peace. In addition to all this, take up the shield of faith, with which you can extinguish all the flaming arrows of the evil one. Take the helmet of salvation and the sword of the Spirit, which is the word of God.

This passage underscores the need to provide military and spiritual warriors with equipment. Pastors' war gear is required to be successful when engaging with the enemy. When David fought Goliath[76] on the battlefield in the valley of Elah, he was armed with

---

[76] I Sam. 17:4.

the Holy Spirit. Joshua battled for the Promised Land with the protection of the Ark of the Covenant.[77] The Bible emphasizes the whole armor of God, not partial armor. Anything less than full armor will weaken the warrior. The specific armaments include the belt of truth, the breastplate of righteousness, the sandals of peace, the shield of faith, the helmet of salvation, the sword of the spirit, and the word of God. John says that the word of God is Jesus himself.

STAGE 7: HOPE/PEACE

We springboard from Stage Six of Faith/Trust to Stage Seven of Hope/Peace. In *The Wounded Healer – Ministry in A Contemporary Society*, Henri J. M. Nouwen addresses the anchor of all human interaction when he says:

> While personal concern is sustained by continuously growing faith in the value of the meaning of life, the deepest motivation for leading our fellow human beings to the future is hope. Hope makes it possible to look beyond the fulfillment of urgent wishes and pressing desires and offers a vision beyond human suffering and death[78] . . . without hope, we will never be able to see value and meaning in the encounter with a decaying human being and become personally concerned. This hope stretches far beyond the limitations of one's psychological strength, for it is anchored not just in the soul of an individual but in God's self-disclosure in history.[79]

Nouwen validates this tenet in the previous narrative. Thus, the Faith/Trust stage becomes the safety net and ushers the reset into the

---

[77] Heb. 9:1-5.
[78] Nouwen, *Wounded Healer*, 81.
[79] Nouwen, *Wounded Healer*, 82.

final stage of Hope/Peace. When all else is lost, the only thing left is hope. Hope gives pastors the incentive to carry on. In "An Essay on Man," Alexander Pope says, "Hope springs eternal in the human breast; Man, never is, but always to be blest. The soul, uneasy and confined from home, Rests and expatiates in a life to come."[80]

COMMENTARY ON PSALM 150:1-6.

> <u>Psalm 150:1-6</u>: Praise God in his sanctuary; praise him in his mighty heavens. Praise him for his mighty acts of power and his surpassing greatness. Praise him with the trumpet sounding, praise him with the harp and lyre, praise him with timbrel and dancing, praise him with strings and pipe, praise him with the clash of cymbals, praise him with resounding cymbals. Let everything that has breath praise the Lord. Praise the Lord.

This passage is a source of hope and peace, for it tells of a mighty God in the heavens. When pastors journey through the seven stages of reset and come full circle, they will arrive at a place of solitude and tranquility. Pastors' confidence will return now that they have returned to the center of God's Will. A pastor's vocation will be validated again with renewed hope in the calling to the ministry to proclaim the gospel to a darkened and lonely world.

Pastors will find the light that resonates in them in the person of Jesus Christ. This hope will yield to peace, and their spirits will soar in song and praise to the God who called them. In this stage, their Shalom will turn to joy. Then they will join the chorus singing, "Let everything that has breath praise the Lord."

---

[80] Alexander Pope, "An Essay on Man," https://goodreads.com/quotes/10692-hope-springs-eternal-in-the-human-breast-man-never-is.

Commentary on John 10:7-10.

<blockquote>

John 10:7-10: Then Jesus said to them again, "Most assuredly, I say to you, I am the door of the sheep. All who came before Me were thieves and robbers, but the sheep did not hear them. I am the door. If anyone enters by Me, he will be saved and will go in and out and find pasture. The thief does not come except to steal, kill, and destroy; I have come that they may it more abundantly.

</blockquote>

Hope enters the lives of pastors to give them renewed energy. It restores, refreshes, and resets wounded clergies. God does not limit the abundance He has planned for the laborers in his vineyard. Jesus is the door to this renewal and reset. Although the roaring lion continues to prowl, thieves and robbers will not go away; they cannot penetrate the sheepfold as long as the Good Shepherd is tending the flock. This passage gives hope that pastors will be protected, knowing every pastor will be counted. When a pastor gets lost, Jesus, the Good Shepherd, will search him out, find him, and bring him back to the fold. Upon returning to the sheepfold, their lives will be abundant again.

Commentary on Romans 8:36-39.

<blockquote>

Romans 8:36-39: As it was written: For Your sake, we are killed all day long; We are accounted as sheep for the slaughter. Yet, in all these things, we are more than conquerors through him who loved us. For I am persuaded that neither death nor life, nor angels nor principalities nor powers, nor things present nor things to come, nor height nor depth, nor any other created thing, shall be able to separate us from the love of God which is in Christ Jesus our Lord.

</blockquote>

This verse fits the battlefield symbolism in this book. Without a doubt, clerics engage in spiritual warfare. Battles include political and military components, evident as much in Paul's time as now. Paul was a veteran of many wars, both physical and spiritual. He speaks with the power of God. He met the King on the road to Damascus, and his wisdom could have been known only from his first-hand experience with God. Paul writes that he is persuaded that he is on the right side of this battle. He confirms that all clergies are embedded with God and that His love will never leave them.

Commentary on Colossians 3:15-17.

> Colossians 3:15-17: Let the peace of Christ rule in your hearts since you were called to peace as members of one body. And be thankful. Let the message of Christ dwell among you richly as you teach and admonish one another with all wisdom through psalms, hymns, and songs from the Spirit, singing to God with gratitude in your hearts. And whatever you do, whether in word or deed, do it all in the name of the Lord Jesus, giving thanks to God the Father through him.

This verse could be a mission statement for Slains Ministries. It reminds pastors that they are members of one body and are called to be at peace with one another. It also teaches wounded pastors that they, as Christian leaders are to teach and admonish one another, holding each other accountable. They are called to lift up each other. Through renewing their minds and hearts, pastors can recite Psalms, sing hymns and praise songs, and pray with gratitude from their hearts. In all their methods of worship, they are to acknowledge Him in the name of the Lord Jesus Christ.

Rev. Dr. Donald R. Hayes, DTh DMin

Commentary on John 16:31-33.

> <u>John 16:31-33</u>: Jesus answered them, "Do you now believe? Indeed, the hour is coming, yes, that you will be scattered each to his own and will leave Me alone. And yet I am not alone because the father is with Me. These things I have spoken to you, that you may have peace in Me. You will have tribulation in the world: but be of good cheer, for I have overcome the world."

Many pastors say they were not fully prepared for their ministries. Some enter this vocation with unrealistic expectations. Some enter on their own accord rather than by a calling from God. A huge number sought ordination to escape the draft during the Vietnam War. This may explain why so many clerics are falling away from this vocation. John clearly states that the ministry is not for the faint. Jesus says that ministers will face trials and tribulations in their lives.

This is not related to clerics only. The laity will have their share of troubles. This verse provides peace because Jesus has overcome the world, which means he has battled for the faithful and won. Ministers should take heart that although many may lose skirmishes along their journeys, the ultimate battle that counts has already been won.

Commentary on Ephesians 5:1-4.

> <u>Ephesians 5:1-4</u>: Therefore, be imitators of God as dear children. And walk in love, as Christ has loved us and given Himself for us, an offering and a sacrifice to God for a sweet-smelling aroma. But fornication and all uncleanness or covetousness, let it not even be named among you, as is fitting for saints; neither filthiness, foolish talking, nor coarse jesting, which are

not fitting, but rather giving of thanks. For this, you know that no fornicator, unclean person, or covetousness man who is an idolator has any inheritance in the kingdom of God.

God tells pastors to be imitators of Him, not of the evil in the world. God says if a pastor looks at the world like a child by giving complete trust in Him, they will walk in love as Christ commanded. The takeaway from this lesson is to be yourself. Pastors begin the healing process if they are honest with themselves. Finding clarity is problematic because it takes pastors to places filled with past grievances and pain. Nevertheless, this trail must be traveled if the pastor expects to reach a place of complete refreshment and restoration. As clay in the potter's hands, clerics need to travel through the seven reset stages and come full circle to a place of respite and rest. Here, clerics will find hope and peace in the hands of God.

Commentary of Philippians 4:10-13.

Philippians 4:10-13: But rejoice in the Lord greatly that bow, at last, your care for me has flourished again: though you indeed did care, you lacked opportunity. Not that I speak regarding need, for I have learned in whatever state I am in to be content: I know how to be abased, and I know how to abound. Everywhere and in all things, I have learned to be complete and hungry; both abound and suffer need. I can do all things through Christ who strengthens me.

Paul may best exemplify the pattern for the lives of pastors. Paul had the world as his footstool. He was a Roman citizen. He was a wise rabbi. He had the best of both worlds, Roman and Hebrew. Yet, he cast it all aside to serve the Messiah. This is the same commitment pastors are called to make in their ordinations. Clerics are expected to adapt to their stations in life, whatever that station may be. It could be in a thriving congregation or a poor rural parish. In either scenario and all points in between, Jesus says He is in their midst wherever two or three are gathered.

This is a great challenge for most clergy because all expect to serve successful churches when they enter the seminary. The definition of success can mean different things to different people. If significant numbers are desired, a large church attendance is the answer. If numerous baptisms are needed, then that will define their success.

However, the results could be much better. Learning to be content may be the hardest lesson clergies must learn. It requires accepting what God has planned for each minister, not what each minister believes God has prepared for him. Not every priest becomes a bishop, nor every deacon becomes a priest. There are many parts to the body of the church, and it takes all parties to work in unison for the church to be alive and well.

Commentary on Ephesians 4:25-32.

> Ephesians 4:25-32: Therefore, putting away lying, let each of you speak the truth with his neighbor, for we are members of one another. Be angry, and do not sin; do not let the sun go down on your wrath, nor give place to the devil. Let him who stole steal no longer, but rather let him labor, working with his hands what is good, that he may have something to give him who has need. Let no corrupt word proceed out of your mouth, but what is good for necessary edification, that it may impart grace to the hearers while letting all bitterness, wrath, anger, clamor, and evil speaking be put away from you, with all malice. And be kind to one another, tenderhearted, forgiving one another, even as God in Christ forgave you.

This last passage sums up this chapter on the biblical basis of this book. Like all believers, pastors are expected to present themselves as holy and acceptable unto God. One Pastoral Care, Inc. statistic noted in chapter one is that many people misrepresent the truth daily. This includes pastors. Not telling the whole truth is the same as lying. Pastors must be honest with themselves before being honest with the people around them. Pastors must have contempt for sin and call it when they see it. They should not harbor wrath; if they do, they need to address it with whoever is the target before the sun goes down on that day. If contempt continues the next day, it is like cancer that will grow until it is unstoppable.

Additionally, pastors should set an example in their actions, words, and deeds by avoiding nasty comments from their mouths. Pastors must extend grace as much as possible but not cave to the world's pressures. Pastors must be firm in their exhortations. Evil must be separated from pastors and replaced with gentleness and kindness. Finally, pastors must learn to forgive because Jesus says if we cannot forgive, how can we expect our Father to forgive us?

In summary, the first stage is the fall from grace. The following five stages are the battles that must be fought and won. The sixth stage is the safety net, while the seventh stage is the recovery and reset. This Seven Stages of Reset has been developed as a training and learning tool for Slains Ministries. Chapter Three will discuss the seven battlefields clergy face in their ministries.

CHAPTER THREE

Theaters of Conflict

The Seven Stages of Reset

This chapter will observe the theaters of conflict where the minister wages daily battles. Pastors are the modern-day stormtroopers[81] like their German military namesake. They are trained to withstand sudden assaults and engage in continuous fighting. They are at a greater risk since they are called to be examples of righteousness for the faithful. Thus, they are high-value targets for evil to attack. Often, evil makes a frontal or rear assault when it is least expected. These battles are usually emotionally and spiritually exhausting.

However, spiritual warfare can become refreshing and renewing to the spirit when victory is won. The previous chapter described the seven stages of reset from the biblical perspective. This chapter will view the battlefield from a personal perspective. Pastors must guard their flanks to prevent losing their effectiveness caused by their sin due to a fallen nature. These identified conflict areas may underscore why many pastors leave their churches and ministries regularly.

---

[81] "Storm Trooper Definition & Meaning" – Dictionary.com. https://www.dictionary.com>browse.

These seven reset stages align with the seven theaters of conflict where clerics are pushed to their limits. They are significant battlegrounds that Slains Ministries expects to address in their recovery and reset therapies. The Seven-Stage Reset Therapy is a creation of Slains Ministries for their counseling modules. It is a first-of-its-kind product based on years of practical and clinical experience. They represent many therapies that are condensed into these seven stages. These modules will provide an overview of the problems clerics face and help them reset and recover. These seven theaters of conflict include the following: 1) Range of the Battlefield - Pride/Vanity, 2) Enemy Within - Doubt/Depression, 3) Luminous Battle - Temptation/Addiction, 4) Fog of War - Guilt/Despair, 5) Battlefield Strategy – Fear/Anxiety, 6) Battle Plan - Faith/Trust, and 7) Battle for Victory - Hope/Peace.

These seven battlefields were first developed as part of an independent research project. This chapter will expand on them since they are a foundational part of Slains Ministries. They will provide the blueprint for recovery, restoration, and reset. They are written under the umbrella of the ultimate battle described in Revelation. It will show how clergy must prepare to face the forces of evil in an increasingly decaying and spiritually declining world.

Yet, through the sequential seven stages of the reset process, the wounded warrior can survive to claim victory. Although conflicts are unpleasant, they are inevitable since they mirror the self-centered world in which humanity exists and engages in the marketplace. These battles will continue as long as humankind seeks power, prestige, and pleasure.

The common desire of most believers is to live in a blissful world without the conflicts inherent in life's struggle with the things of heaven versus the things of earth. This outlook often causes many to look longingly at the past and wish the present was different. Many ask, "What if?" "Why, Lord?" or "Why did God allow this tragedy?"[82] Whether or not these questions are answered is up to the

---

[82] Jonathon Sacks, "*Why Does God Allow Terrible Things to Happen to His People?*" *The Chesterton Review* 34, no. ½ (2008): 367-370.

reader and the participant in Slains Ministries. Thus, this study aims to guide the wounded pastors through these seven battlefields and provide tools to navigate life's most challenging problems.

The Christian's faith in God will be at the heart of this study. As mentioned, its aim is to develop a three-day clergy-care center to help spiritually wounded clergy reset their calling and ministries. This objective is crucial since strong leadership in battle is the key to shepherding believers through this world's challenges.

A three-part approach to healing is envisioned for pastors and will provide 1) spiritual comfort, 2) mental stability, and 3) well-being for the body. It encompasses the metaphysical and tripartite nature of man's being. Pastors will focus on items that lift the spirit, like music and art, receive spiritual counseling, and experience healthy physical activity. Experts in each field will be summoned to help wounded clergies reset their priorities and reclaim the spirit of their calling.

Military Bearing

In the military world, providing soldiers and sailors with a respite from the front lines of battle is vital to a healthy fighting force. The United States military has incorporated this treatment in its battle plans for decades. Since WWII, combatants have been regularly deployed away from the front lines for a few days of respite to reset their bodies, mind, and spirit. These regular intervals are called R&R, an acronym for rest and relaxation. Jesus knew the importance of keeping a fighting force healthy when he said, "The harvest is plentiful, but the workers are few; therefore, pray earnestly to the Lord of the harvest to send out laborers into his harvest." [83]

Although the completion of spiritual healing is a process that may take months or years to reach fruition, at least the process has begun. The Seven-Step Reset will redirect the wounded clergy toward a desired and thriving destination. Slain's mission is to return

---

[83] Vaughn Roberts, *Workers for the Harvest Field* (Surrey UK: The Good Book Company, 2012), Introduction.

the spiritual warrior to the battlefield stronger than before attending the retreat.

Historical Perspective

A view from the battlefield must include a historical perspective to fully understand the inherent challenges because history is said to repeat itself. Such an implicit mission is a reminder that there is nothing new under the sun.[84] The church has routinely been at odds over theology, method of worship, and dogma. Many observers believe that healing the divisions in the church would lead to the healing of clerics.

Splits or schisms have occurred regularly for centuries and have always divided the church. The first significant split occurred when the Western Church split with the Eastern Church, causing the Great Schism in 1054. The last major split occurred when the Western Church separated from Rome during the Protestant Reformation[85] five hundred years later. This split began in Wittenberg, Germany, in 1517 and continued for decades. In 1534, the Church of England separated from Rome, as did subsequent Protestant denominations. The historians who share this view conclude that the turmoil ended somewhere between the Peace of Augsburg in 1555, which allowed for the coexistence of Catholicism and Lutheranism in Germany, and the 1648 Treaty of Westphalia, which ended the Thirty Years War.

While unity is much desired, some say another split is brewing within the Western Church. If true, what would the 21st-century church look like at a similar turning point? The Episcopal Church ended a ten-year court battle with one of its dioceses where the church was damaged. Now, the United Methodist Church is going through similar disruptions. The following battlefields will address some of these challenges.

---

[84] Eccles. 1:9.
[85] "The Reformation" History Channel.com, https://www.history.com>topics>reformation.

The church has tried to ward off further splits and remain unified. Great church councils took place in the past but continue to have lingering effects today. Many Christian principles were addressed, including infant baptism, the Trinity of God, and Holy Communion.

For historical purposes of inclusion, the subsequent great gatherings are listed as follows: the First Council of Nicaea in 325, the First Council of Constantinople in 381, the Council of Ephesus in 431, the Council of Chalcedon in 451, the Second Council in Constantinople in 533, the Third Council of Constantinople from 680-681 and the Second Council of Nicaea in 787. In each council, the Christian church yielded to the events of its day. Whether biblical principles were diminished is a matter of continuous debate.

Council Comparisons

Historical councils include the Council of Trent from 1545 to 1563, Vatican I from 1869 to 1870, and Vatican II from 1962 to 1965. It is important to note that church leaders assemble irregularly to settle differences in church polity[86] and dogma. However, it is not uncommon for denominational councils to meet at regular intervals. The General Convention of the Southern Baptists meets annually in Nashville, Tennessee, while the Lambeth Council of the Anglican Communion, convened by the Archbishop of Canterbury, meets every ten years in London, England.

Challenges to the church's doctrine and dogma occur primarily because the church's mission is to uphold the gospel in a secular world. Popular culture is the source driving today's divisions in the church. Knowing the history of church conflict helps wounded pastors gain an understanding and perspective in their ministries. This provides a foundation for the healing process moving forward through the professional assistance provided by Slains Ministries.

---

[86] *"Meaning and Modernity: Religion, Polity, and Self."* Edited by Richard Madsen, William M. Sullivan, Ann Swidler, and Steven M. Tipton. (Berkeley: University of California Press, 2002), Introduction, X.

Biblical scholars have debated the nuances of religious and denominational differences for centuries. On par, denominational differences have been respectful in terms of method of worship. Many communities share clergy alliances. As Soldiers for Christ, it is essential that despite the various views, Christians have a common enemy in evil, not each other. Thus, pastors and laity should save their artillery for the true enemy.

The Seven War Zones

Theater of conflict is another description of war zones. When wounded clerics are trained to recognize and understand these various theaters, they can learn to avoid them. These spiritual warriors are no different from military warriors. The only difference is the range of weapons used to battle their enemies. This chapter will outline the seven battlefields of which clergy must be aware. These theaters of conflict are listed in the following sequential stages.

Since Christians are called to live in this world yet not be a part of it, this opens the door to naiveté. It is a delicate balancing act. How far one will venture into the unknown is the question. It is paramount that all pastors understand that everything seen cannot be unseen, and everything heard cannot be unheard. This is why Jesus said that believers should be harmless as doves yet wise as serpents.[87] This contrast is compared to someone with street sense versus book sense. A dose of common sense will benefit a pastor. Gaining that knowledge is no easy matter.

Stage One – Range of the Battlefield – Pride/Vanity

This battlefield is worldwide. Christian pastors are on every continent, and their challenges will affect ministers everywhere. Slains Ministry can grow internationally. Therefore, this book will develop a blueprint that can be offered here and abroad. The blueprint or

---
[87] Matt. 10:16.

field manual will be offered as a source of empirical therapy for any Christian pastor who needs help. However, the Slains Seven Stage Reset will be proprietary and copyrighted.

In the research stage of development, it was discovered that the seven-stage reset therapies could be helpful to groups outside of clerics. Many professionals other than clergy are at risk of burnout because professionals from other disciplines are under a great deal of stress. Society represents social creatures who engage with each other in various types of businesses. Those institutions include economic, commercial, medical, military, industrial, manufacturing, and educational organizations. And yet, they face similar challenges of job-related stress and burnout. It reflects the more significant battle, not against principalities and powers, but the larger forces of darkness and light. The final struggle leads to the eternal conflict between Heaven and Hell. Many souls are at stake for eternal destiny and are not limited to clergies.

The range of the battlefield is not limited to just geographical boundaries, but it is historical and chronological. The enemy is a stealthy[88] target. The spiritual soldier will likely find himself on the defensive rather than the offensive. The forces of evil know the stakes are high and will cast every possible deception and false narrative against the forces of good.

This tactic causes a destabilizing effect. The recent cancel culture movement, which limits freedom of speech, is an excellent example of the battlefield. The spiritual soldier's challenge thus lies in taking the fight to the enemy. One way to win the battle is to confront the enemy head-on, evangelize to the lost, and proclaim the Gospel without reservation or apology.

Many believe that the organized church made a mistake when it cozied up to the culture, causing the gospel's truth to become opaque. Like politicians and special interest groups, the church has forged an

---

[88] Binayak Pattanaik and Aditya Chauhan, "A Study of Stealth Technology," *Materials Today,* Proceedings. May 3, 2021.

unholy alliance validated by the phrase "Sleeping with the enemy."[89] People outside the church see clerics and believers as hypocritical.

The denominational church has allowed evil to become its friend, not her enemy. For instance, many church followers misconstrue the brick-and-mortar buildings and call it the church, while God knows the church is made up of her flesh and blood, true believers.

Church Conflicts

Many churches have adopted secular business practices, where performance and reward replace grace and mercy. Well-funded churches witness infighting between pastors for coveted church assignments. These assignments include addictive salaries and perks on par with temporal business models, which can cause spiritual wounds. This behavior causes harm from within and is known in military circles as friendly fire. These highly sought-after church positions are typically reserved for ring members, as C.S. Lewis describes in *The Weight of Glory*.[90] As a result, this adds pressure on the clergy and expands the range of the battlefield.

The systemic pressure on clergy is compounded as scandals in the past few decades have weakened the church's authority and created a deep distrust within society. These past grievances tend to linger and build up over time until their situation becomes untenable. These past grievances often are carried over to the new pastor, who has to face the fallout, although it was no fault on his part. Then, clergy, reacting to past pain and suffering, become their own worst enemy. When wounded clergy fall from grace, it becomes a public spectacle. The media celebrate the demise and proclaim it as a rule,

---

[89] Miguel Espinosa, Akhil Ilango, and Giorgio Zanarone. "*Sleeping with the Enemy: How Politicians and Interest Groups Adapt their Collaborations in the Face of Reputational Threats,*" Preprint, submitted in 2022, https://www.researchgate.net/publication/361017862_Sleeping_with_the_Enemy_How_Politicians_and_Interest_Groups_Adapt_their_Collaborations_in_the_Face_of_Reputational_Threats/link/6297d8886886635d5cb5ad2e/download.

[90] Clive Staples Lewis, *The Weight of Glory* (Grand Rapids: Zondervan, 2001), 144.

not an exception. The fall from grace of several televangelists adds fuel to the fire and adds to the cracks in the church's foundation. This could have been the cause of churches' declining attendance for several decades.

An example of this type of fracture occurred in the Anglican world when, in 2003, the Episcopal bishop of New Hampshire, the Rt. Rev. Vicky Eugene Robinson divorced his wife and established a domestic partnership with his homosexual cohort. Numerous other reported denominational travails occurred, including the rampant pedophilia reported in the Roman Catholic Church. Recently, the media, under the Freedom of Information Statute, forced the Southern Baptist Convention to address the decades-long behavior of sexual misconduct by their clergy. These battlefield losses will cause long-term pain and suffering and adversely affect families for generations. These blatant displays of internal conflict undermine the church's tenets and exponentially complicate the battle for the lost and lonely. Scripture addresses these unabashed sideshows in Psalms: "So I gave them over to their stubborn hearts to follow their own devices."[91]

STAGE TWO – ENEMY WITHIN – DOUBT/DEPRESSION

This theater transitions clerics who fall from grace due to pride and vanity. This predicament leads to a period of doubt and depression. Pastors seek more clarity about their calling, vocation, and ministry and face doubts about themselves. This can lead to a state of melancholy, and in severe cases, depression can set in, which, like Post Traumatic Stress[92], can lead to a debilitating disorder. In these cases, pastors become paralyzed and have difficulty functioning in everyday activities like personal hygiene and adequate rest and exercise. Here, pastors enter a period of self-analysis and introspection. In worst-case scenarios, they question the existence of God. Then, anger and

---

[91] Ps. 81:12.
[92] Rachael Yehuda, "Post-Traumatic Stress Disorder," _New England Journal of Medicine_, 346, no. 2 (2002): 108-114.

a sense of betrayal and abandonment evolve in the mind and heart of the pastor.

Stage One noted how the organized church essentially had become prey to the culture. Thus, the clerics become their prey. When the pastors succumb to the pressures, so can the church body. When this happens, the door opens for doubt and depression on the part of both clergy and laity. Many of today's churches have become a place for entertainment, not worship. Many believers with good intentions have steered the church away from prayer and taken worship into an unholy alliance between church and culture. Worshipping things other than God can lead to this kind of battlefield. This behavior leads in the wrong direction, and it's not heaven.

Indeed, the Holy Scripture addresses this concern about the gate to Heaven. Jesus says, "Strive to enter through the narrow gate, for many, I say to you, will seek to enter and will not be able."[93] Another passage talks about a stranger not wearing his wedding robe entering the banquet. This reflects the message from the fable of a "Wolf in Sheep's Clothing,"[94] where "Many Are Called, But Few Are Chosen."[95] This verse makes pastors question if God chose them for the ministry. This causes pastors suffering from depression to question everything, including their salvation.

Pastors must remember that Jesus said, "We May Live in This World, But We Are Called Out of This World."[96] In other words, believers must find a way to coexist in a non-Christian counterculture.[97] Jesus, the Messiah, faced the same predicament and was deemed a revolutionary. This is evident by what the Pharisees and Sadducees said about him in the Gospels. They believed that he was an imposter sent to destroy their world. He did, but the status

---

[93] Luke 13:24.
[94] *A Wolf in Sheep's Clothing Definition*, *Cambridge English Dictionary*. dictionary.cambridge.org.
[95] Matt. 12:14.
[96] Ben Witherington III, *Jesus, Paul, and the End of the World* (Vestmont: Intervarsity Press, 1992), 26.
[97] Larry Eskridge. *God's Forever Family: The Jesus People Movement in America* (New York: Oxford University Press USA, 2013), 10.

quo survived. Jesus said he came to save the world, not to destroy it. He came to fulfill the law and the prophets.[98] He came to create a culture focused on God and not the world, the flesh, and the devil. The same evil enemy has plagued humanity since Adam and Eve's days in the Garden of Eden.

A familiar quotation is recorded on the website BookBrowse, "You Can Run, But You Cannot Hide."[99] This lesson teaches pastors to get right with God. A relationship built on trust will be sustainable in the heat of battle. Temptation is around every corner, and it will weaken the minister's relationship with Almighty God.

Facing a weakened spiritual nature makes a pastor stronger if he turns his focus on God. Paul says, "For when I am weak, then I am strong."[100] As Christian soldiers fighting the battle of truth versus evil, it is God's battle to win. Jesus says, "I am the vine; you are the branches. Whoever abides in me and I in him, he it is that bears much fruit, for apart from me, you can do nothing."[101] This translates that everyone is more incredible with God.

THE ENEMY

Many think that outside enemies should be jailed, terminated, or should reach some early demise by the public executioner or by an act of God. But how do pastors address the enemy within? The paradox for believers is inherent in the words of Jesus Christ, who teaches us to pray for and love our enemies.[102] This includes praying for ourselves. The enemy within becomes "Our Own Worst Enemy."[103] The greatest enemy within is deception. We are plagued

---

[98] Matt. 5:17.
[99] BookBrowse.com/expressions/detail/index.cfm/expression_number/238/you-can-run-but-you-can't-hide.
[100] 2 Cor. 12:10.
[101] John 15:5.
[102] John Nolland, "The Mandate: Love Our Enemies Matt. 5:43-48." *Anvil 21*, no. 1 (2004): 23.
[103] James Montier. *The Little Book of Behavioral Investing: How Not to Be Your Worst Enemy*, Vol. 35. (New York: John Wiley & Sons, 2010) Cover.

by the seven deadly sins of pride, greed, lust, envy, gluttony, wrath, and sloth.[104] The fact that these seven sins are led by pride gives credence to the dominance pride has on us and opens the door to the other sins. Pride becomes the gateway to sin. It has been said that "Pride Goes Before The Fall." On YouTube, for instance, searching for the phrase "False Preachers" reveals that pride opened the door to the fall of many televangelists.

Brother Against Brother

In Genesis, we read the story of Cain and Abel, where the former slew his brother. Further, we read of the brokenness between Jacob and Esau or the dysfunctional relationship between Saul and David. Throughout history, there has been a constant ebb and flow of heroes and villains, blessings and curses, kingdoms, and principalities; all demonstrated in the world of good and evil. This is the world everyone, especially pastors, must navigate daily.

God tells us that the battle of good versus evil begins in the hearts of men. In Ephesians, we read, "For our struggle is not against flesh and blood, but against the rulers, against the authorities, against the powers of this dark world and spiritual forces of evil in heavenly realms."[105] If soldiers of the cross succumb to the world, the flesh, and the devil, they become the realm's enemies. Thus, they fail to find the solution to the enemy within.

Be Strong and Courageous

Jesus cautions against the evil that can overtake us. We must guard against the pride that can envelop and corrupt our hearts and minds. When we become prideful or boastful and fail to give God credit, we become self-righteous hypocrites. We risk becoming refuse on the battlefield. Then, like the tares on the threshing floor, we

---

[104] Solomon Schimmel. "The Seven Deadly Sins: Jewish, Christian, and Classical Reflections on Human Psychology." (Oxford: Oxford University Press, 1997.)
[105] Eph. 6:12.

become useful in as much as giving fuel to the fire. Jesus distinguishes between the wheat and the tares. Wheat is made into bread and sustains life, while tares are useless and are cast into the fiery pit.[106]

Forgiveness

We must learn to forgive. If we do not forgive, it becomes like cancer that can destroy the wounded clergy. Jesus said, "If you cannot forgive others, how can you expect my Father to forgive you?"[107] Ironically, forgiveness is thought by many to be one of the most challenging lessons to learn in Christian theology. On the cross, Jesus says, "Father, forgive them, for they know not what they do."[108] This is an example of the depth of God's love and forgiveness. This kind of forgiveness destroys our enemies.

Much of the Christian experience is rooted in the decisions about God and each other. When the public maligns or injures others, their hearts become hardened, and they find it difficult to forgive. Scripture teaches that a believer cannot have a heart of stone. Believers must be motivated by an intrinsic desire for the well-being of others.[109] Thus, an unforgiving heart cannot be a part of a Christian soldier's arsenal. Everyone faces pain at some juncture in life. This pain can lead to trauma. Michael and Kathy Langston say in their devotional:

> Trauma provides us with deep spiritual, physical, and emotional pain. Escaping the pain is not always the goal of our Heavenly Father. We, like Jesus, can glorify God if we surrender to His will for our lives. We can find the purpose

---

[106] Matt. 13:24-30.
[107] Jared P. Pingleton, "Why We Don't Forgive: A Biblical and Object Relations Theoretical Model for Understanding Failures in The Forgiveness Process." *Journal of Psychology and Theology* 25, no. 4 (1997). 403-413.
[108] Luke 23:24.
[109] Anne W. Stewart, "Moral Agency in the Hebrew Bible," *Oxford Research Encyclopedia of Religion*. 2016. 106.

for being on this earth through the leadership of the Holy Spirit. Pain can be how we find our way into a deeper relationship with God.[110]

The same God who melts ice is the same one who hardens clay. Further, in Hannah's prayer,[111] God makes poor the ones he does not make wealthy. He is the author of both life and death. This leaves room in the equation for choice. Ultimately, humanity must decide between the forces of life and death. In his comic strip Pogo, Walt Kelly says:[112] "We Have Met the Enemy, And He Is Us."

If Christian soldiers are to wage war against evil on the battlefield of faith, they must start by overcoming the enemy from within. Looking in a mirror exposes pastors to their actual personas. An honest approach to the things that need repair or reset is the beginning of the road to healing. Not being completely transparent with us is a recipe for failure. The recovery period begins by getting to the root of the problem that brought the minister to his breaking point.

STAGE THREE – LUMINOUS BATTLE - TEMPTATION/ADDICTION

Shakespeare says: "All That Glitters Is Not Gold."[113] The attraction for fame and fortune is a magnet for much of the world. It is a trap that many have fallen into by chasing this proverbial pot of gold. Much like the Enemy Within Stage are the wonders, desires, and dreams of the heart and imaginations of the mind. Such is the framework of the Luminous Battle, which occurs internally, in contrast to the Fog of War in Stage Four, which forms externally.

---

[110] Michael W. Langston and Kathy J. Langston, *From Despair to Hope* (Silverton: Lampion Press, 2017), 99.
[111] 2 Sam. 2:1-10.
[112] Walt Kelly. *We Have Met the Enemy, And He Is Us* (New York: Simon and Shuster, 1972). Cover.
[113] All That Glitters Is Not Gold Meaning & Context of Quote. No Sweat Shakespeare. https://nosweatshapeakespers.com. Assessed May 4, 2023.

Pastors must take stringent precautions and guard against the web of evil which plagues the battlefield. The Christian soldier should be prepared for every obstacle that the enemy employs, who, as a roaring lion,[114] is out to devour anyone in its path. In this battle stage, temptation and addiction take center stage. Clerics face the seduction of evil, which is a luminous enemy. This ominous evil is not the world's guiding light. However, the safety and security from this seductive evil are found in the truth of the Gospel, where faith will not waiver. God's word will not be confused or defeated.

Falsehoods

The luminous enemy is not illuminated at all. Instead, evil is a chameleon whose various inculcations appear to be Jesus Christ, the world's light, but is an imposter. The enemy mimics much of the good in the world, but, in the end, it is the opposite. What makes this powerful force so dangerous is that he takes a portion of the truth, not the whole, and makes it believable. Then, he weaves falsehoods around the subject, setting the trap.

A sample of this type of entrapment is the New Age[115] Prosperity teachings, which have become a part of popular culture for over a generation. It requires a Western view of spirituality that focuses on one's ability and knowledge to accumulate worldly possessions to be spiritually fulfilled. Many televangelists tout it as sound doctrine, yet it is riddled with heresy.[116] The enemy is a master of twisting the truth. Evil forces exploit untutored minds and bank on their sloth to develop a perceived knowledge of God and his Word.

---

[114] Sarah Keyes." Like a Roaring Lion: The Overland Trail as a Sonic Quest," *Journal of American History* 96, no.1 (2009), 19-43.

[115] Wouter J. Hanegraaff. *New Age Religion and Western Culture: Esotericism in the Mirror of Secular Thought* (New York: Suny Press, 1997), 49.

[116] *Alister McGrath. Heresy: A History of Defending the Truth* (New York: Harper Collins Publishers, 2009) 2.

The Battlefield of Faith

Pastors must also be alert to the following Scripture:

> Not everyone who says to me, "Lord, Lord," will enter the kingdom of heaven, but only the one who does the will of my Father who is in heaven. Many will say to me on that day, "Lord, did we not prophesy in your name and in your name drive out demons and, in your name, perform many miracles?" Then I will tell them plainly, "I never knew you. Away from me, you evildoers!"[117]

Following the tenets of Christianity requires an effort to establish a genuine relationship with the world's true light, Jesus Christ.

Parable of the Ten Virgins

Speaking of sloth, Jesus used riddles to explain the tenets of truth. This is the biblical story of five wise virgins who had their oil lamps full while five foolish virgins' lamps were empty of oil. The master unexpectedly returned after a long season, so the five foolish virgins asked the five wise virgins to share their oil with them. The five wise virgins refused, and the five without were sent to the marketplace to gather oil for their lamps. In the interim, the bridegroom returned, and those with their lamps filled entered the wedding banquet, and the door behind them was sealed. The five foolish virgins returned, knocking on the door and demanding, "Lord, open the door to us!" But the master replied, "Truly, I tell you, I do not know you."[118] Wounded clergy are well advised to be prepared and watch for the day and the hour when the high command will return.

This parable symbolizes the wise virgins as believers, while the foolish virgins are depicted as unbelievers. When pastors' lamps (hearts

---

[117] Matt. 7:21-23.
[118] Matt. 25:12.

and minds) are empty, they succumb to evil and temptation. Their souls, like lamps, must be filled with the Holy Spirit, not partially. When the bridegroom says he does not know them, he means they know of him, but he does not know them. This distinction is an example of the luminous enemy. The world knows Jesus as a historical figure, a biblical character, or a man who died on the cross. But to know Him and for him to know who believes in him is the only way through the narrow gate of heaven.

Five of the ten virgins had fallen prey to one of the seven deadly sins of sloth. They had become lazy. In a way, they had become addicted to their way of life. Addictions can take hold in many shapes and sizes. Sloth is not generally considered an addiction until closer inspection. Addictions to drugs and alcohol get most of the attention, but we should consider for a moment the habits of the way of the world. Idol worship, love of money, and gluttony are sins. Is that not an addiction? When one lives in a dream world, a luminous world without wants and a world of riches, it leads to an open world of addiction to things that separate wounded spiritual warriors from God.

Stage Four – Fog of War – Guilt/Despair

One can become lost if not connected to God in this fourth theater. Exiting out of temptation and addiction leads to guilt and despair. At this moment, grief and guilt are the pastor's constant companions. With all the sounds and distractions, the world can cause many to lose sight of the ultimate mission to proclaim the gospel of Jesus Christ. In stage three, the biblical lesson was described where the master tells the five virgins whose lamps were empty, "I never knew you."[119] In earnest, our vessels must be Spirit-filled. Pastors who are not connected to Jesus become workers of iniquity. Staying connected to God is like being tied to a tether, where God is holding the opposite end.

---

[119] Mary Ellen Pereira. "I Never Knew You: Jesus' Rebuke in Matthew 7:23," *Leaven 16,* no. 4, 2008, 5.

Jesus warns, "For false Christs and false prophets will rise and show great signs and wonders to deceive, if possible, even the elect."[120] This is a warning for all soldiers of Christ. Jesus adds, "I know that after I leave, savage wolves will come among you and not spare the flock. Even from your number, men will arise and distort the truth to draw away disciples after them."[121] The military calls these men traitors. Pastors must also be aware that spies in their churches report falsehoods to the church hierarchy.

The enemy is identifiable since they do not bear the fruit of the spirit. Although, as the Parable of the Wheat and Tares teaches us, the enemy can appear perfect. They look, act, and sound like sheep but are wolves in sheep's clothing. The enemy's fruit is substandard and not of the soul, while believers' fruit reaches abundant goodness. This litmus test of great fruit helps the spiritual soldier see clearly through the fog of war.

THE ENEMY'S ARSENAL

The enemy's arsenal feeds the dreams and imaginations of clergy's hearts and minds. These external forces attract the eyes, ears, smell, or touch. These are idols of a utopian world to which clergies and laity are drawn. Creatures succumb to worldly desires, believing they are as valuable as gold. Belatedly, it is discovered that they are no more than pyrite, an imposter, which is called fool's gold.[122] Since they are not pure gold, the lesson learned is that all that glitters is not gold.

In and out of the pastorate, all people face times of guilt, grief, or despair. David fled from King Saul after their relationship took a wrong turn when King Saul could not contain his contempt and jealousy for the future king. From David's torment, good came when he wrote the Psalms we enjoy today. God uses our sufferings to magnify his glory. His son Jesus is a prime example. Another example

---

[120] Matt. 24:24.
[121] Matt. 20:29-30.
[122] John MacArthur. *Fool's Gold?* (Wheaton: Crossway Books, 2005), 19.

of grief took place on the night of the Last Supper. The grief Jesus felt when one of his disciples betrayed him. Jesus, being human, must have had some thoughts of guilt for picking his betrayer.

Perhaps the most illustrated form of grief and despair occurred in the Garden of Eden when Jesus said in his prayer, "Father, if you are willing, remove this cup from me; nevertheless, not my will, but thine be done."[123] This grief was so deep that Jesus asked this question three times, and the answer was the same each time. As pastors, we experience doubt, grief, guilt, and despair. Our emotions are intertwined, but God can unravel our situation and provide healing if we let him. Following the time in the Garden of Eden, Jesus was crucified.

On the cross, he said, "Father, forgive them, for they do not know what they are doing."[124] Jesus made peace with his grief and despair. He teaches us to trust in God with all our hearts and minds. As pastors, in all our difficulties, we should do as we learn in Proverb, "Trust in the Lord with all your hearts and lean not in your own understanding; in all your ways acknowledge him, and he will make your paths straight."[125]

GREED

The world's embrace of Hollywood and Wall Street creates many external pitfalls. Many hearts' desires last only for a season, contrasting the hope that worldly treasures last forever. If purchased on credit, one may find they have become enslaved to their creditors, with loan payments lasting several years. Other seductions include addictions to earthly elixirs such as tobacco, drugs, or alcohol.

Pastors facing the world, the flesh, and the devil find it hard to resist its temptations without the solid foundation of a relationship with God and fellow spiritual warriors. The benefit of associating with other pastors reflects on the Biblical passage: "Love and serve

---

[123] Luke 22:42.
[124] Luke 23:34.
[125] Prov. 3:5-6.

one another."[126] This gives strength to the pastor in a world designed to entrap him into Satan's web and lead him away from God.

Peering through the fog of war by comparing and contrasting the metaphysical nature of humanity helps wounded clergy focus on the battlefield. This is accomplished by dissecting the strengths and weaknesses of the enemy. Clerics can approach the battlefield better prepared to engage the enemy and be victorious at this level. Guarding the hearts, minds, and spirits of pastors thwarts the enemies' attempts to deceive them with partial truths and helps to see through the fog of war.

Stage Five – Battlefield Strategy – Fear/Anxiety

The fifth theater of war leads spiritually wounded clergy from guilt/despair to fear/anxiety. This is the most challenging battlefield where the wounded clergy will hit rock bottom. In these anxious moments of despair, clergies will reach a level of fear. In this capacity, pastors will begin to see the face of God. Proverbs say: "The fear of the Lord is the beginning of wisdom, and knowledge of the Holy One is understanding."[127] This downward spiral yields a "j" curve that begins the turn around upward.

Wars are designed for victory. In Revelation, John wrote about the final battle and the victorious outcome. However, getting from here to there will require battlefield strategies. Wounded clerics can take a lesson from the shepherd David, who, facing the menacing Goliath[128] in the Valley of Elah, was prepared to use whatever ordnance he had at his disposal. Pastors need the same skills as David when executing a battle plan. David carefully selected his weapon and refused the heavy sword and cumbersome body armor offered by King Saul. Instead, he used a sling and a rock found in his pouch tied around his waist, which he often used to disperse carnivorous wolves

---

[126] Gal. 5:13.
[127] Prov. 9:10.
[128] Azzan Yadin, "Goliath's Armor and Israelite Collective Memory." *Vetus Testamentum* 54, no. 3 (2004). 373-395.

who attacked his herd of sheep. More importantly, God was at his side and ultimately slew the giant.

Pastors must fulfill God's will to win the battle of good versus evil. The cornerstone of any field strategy is remembering that the battle is God's. Wounded clerics who have been reset are the spiritual warriors God has assembled to fulfill his plan for humanity.

In The Heat of the Battle

War plans are exhilarating because they often unfold differently than planned or expected. There will be twists and turns along the way. Therefore, contingency plans are critical and necessary components for battle preparations. A competent military planner will always have a backup plan. The Bible gives us examples of how we are to engage the enemy. Wartime's leverage is strengthened by the hand of God and is the critical ingredient for victory.

Jesus Christ, the supreme commander, used the parables of Scripture to confront and defeat the enemy. Each time Satan tested him, Jesus quoted or referred to scripture, saying, "It is written." The pastor's main objective is to be well-versed in Scripture to engage and successfully deflect the enemy's slicing swords and piercing arrows.

In *The Pilgrim's Progress*[129], John Bunyan writes a story of the twists and turns of its main character, Christian. He employed wisdom and knowledge to navigate his remarkable journey's many perils confronting him. We compare our journey to his in many ways. Christians should be prepared to change course or pivot midstream and adapt a backup or contingency plan.

When pastors are engaged in the spiritual battle for the hearts and minds of the lost, they must be well-trained. They must be prepared for an enemy who may have more significant numbers. The enemy possesses cunning and deception as a hallmark of his battle plan. One of the deceptions the enemy uses with great success is the element of surprise. So, pastors must be agile enough to adjust while maintaining

---

[129] John Bunyan. *The Pilgrim's Progress* (New York: Barnes & Nobel Classics, 2005), Cover to cover.

the course and sight of the objective. Every commissioned officer or NCO is issued a field manual[130] and expected to know the lessons inherent in this instruction book, much like the Bible.

Road Map

For the Christian soldier, the field manual is the Holy Scriptures. In addition to this book are training and resource manuals consisting of biblical commentaries and Christian publications. They increase the knowledge of the wiles of the evil one. The Christian soldier is also equipped with numerous biblical translations, which supplement his understanding of the enemy and grant him tools to confront the evil in the world. Sound knowledge of these documents will prepare the pastor to "Fight the good fight of faith"[131] as we recall Paul's message in I Timothy.

Two-Edged Sword

Battle strategies are divided into strategic and tactical categories. The strategic or macro plan involves the overall design, while the tactical or micro plan involves implementing strategies in minute detail. One of the strategic objectives for the Christian warrior is a thorough grounding in Christian dogma.[132] In other words, Christian soldiers should know and believe in the foundations of their faith. These foundations include the Apostles' Creed, the Nicene Creed, the Athanasian Creed, and the Catechism of the Church.

Additionally, Christians should adhere to sanctified documents such as the Presbyterian Covenant, the Anglican Thirty-nine Articles of Religion, the Lutheran Confession, and so on. Inherent in these

---

[130] Walter Edward Kretchik. *US Army Doctrine: From the American Revolution to the War on Terror* (Lawrence, KS: University Press of Kansas, 2011), Preface.

[131] Rod Culbertson. *The Disciple Investing Apostle: Paul's Ministry of Relationships Vol. 3* (Eugene: Wipf and Stock Publishers, 2018), 8.

[132] Hans W. Frei. *The identity of Jesus Christ. Expanded and Updated Edition. The Hermeneutical Bases of Dogmatic Theology* (Eugene: Wipf and Stock Publishers, 2013). Introduction.

Protestant and Catholic documents are the beliefs of all Christians. Seminary training is desired where the pastor, priest, elder, and deacon are trained in theology, apologetics, homiletics,[133] and church planting. A knowledge of church history is paramount to the soldier's perspective and understanding of the enemy. Seminars, deanery meetings, and clergy conferences allow soldiers to learn from each other; as the scripture says, "Iron sharpens iron."[134]

Boots on the Ground

The tactical strategy involves "Boots on the ground" or, some say, the "Tip of the spear," where the opposing forces meet face to face. This engagement includes evangelism, witnessing, and attending worship services. It also provides ministries where the tenets of Christianity are applied and integrated into the world through programs that clothe the naked, feed the hungry, and shelter the homeless. This is an outreach ministry for the poor and needy. It occurs along the highways and byways, not in the worship centers. The battle can be fierce at this level, so the stormtroopers or ministers on the front lines must be given ample support to fulfill the missions where they are deployed.

These front-line warriors need R&R[135] regularly to refresh, renew, and restore the required fight. It is strongly recommended that regular sabbaticals[136] are taken to strengthen these fighting forces. Jesus took time in the wilderness to regain his strength. He is the supreme commander, showing pastors how to prepare to defeat the enemy. Once spiritual warriors have endured the trials and

---

[133] Karl Barth. *Homiletics* (Louisville: Westminster John Knox Press, 1991), Preface.

[134] Daniel J. Treier and Uche Anizor, "Theological Interpretation of Scripture and Evangelical Systematic Theology: Iron Sharpening Iron," *Southern Baptist Journal of Theology* 14 (2010): 4-17.

[135] M.R. McMinn, R. Allen Lish, Pamela D. Trice, Alicia M. Root, Nichole Gilbert, and Adelene Yap. "*Care for pastors: Learning from Clergy and Their Spouses,*" *Pastoral Psychology* 53, no. 6 (2005): 563-581.

[136] Richard Bullock and Richard Bruesehoff. *Clergy Renewal: The Alban Guide to Sabbatical Planning* (Washington: Rowan & Littlefield, 2000), 6.

temptations of engaging in evil, they develop a battle rhythm. This cadence keeps the warriors ready, so they don't grow weary and fall in battle.

Battle Tested

A shield to protect pastors from the enemy is called the "Armor of God."[137] InEphesians,[138] Paul says, "For our struggle is not against flesh and blood, but against the rulers, against the authorities, against the powers of this dark world and the spiritual forces of evil in the heavenly realms." Paul writes so that we stand our ground when the day of evil comes. Pastors must buckle the belts around our waists with the truth. Then, they are to robe themselves in the breastplate of righteousness. Next, feet are fitted with the readiness from the gospel of peace.

Finally, pastors are to take up the shield of faith to extinguish the enemy's flaming arrows and crown their heads with the helmet of salvation and the sword of the Spirit, which is the Word of God. The battle is not only of this world. Pastors must prepare battlefield strategies that are ready to complete the victory. Training and equipping front-line troops are the cornerstone of this strategy.

Stage Six – Battle Plan – Faith/Trust

God orchestrates the battle plan. Thus, the sixth theater is the safety net. It shows the importance of a clergy care center called Slains Ministries. This center will be designed as a reset and recovery space and is currently under development. It is hoped to debut as a place of healing for wounded spiritual warriors. The primary objective of Slains Ministries is to care for the clergy in such a way as to keep them engaged in their respective ministries. It is essential to enrich and undergird their spiritual health and well-being.

---

[137] Larry Richards. *The Full Armor of God: Defending Your Life from Satan's Schemes.* (Grand Rapids: Baker Books, 2013), Preface.
[138] Eph. 6:10-18.

This is not to say that the clergymen and women are alone in their calling or struggles. Indeed, spouses and families are just as crucial to a pastor's ministry and need the support a ministry like Slains offers. Initially, Slains Ministries will be designed for clergy, but it is not out of the realm of possibility that, in the future, it will include family members. A spiritually healthy battle force, including support troops like the family, will keep the evil at bay and cast away the roaring lion who is out to devour God's anointed servants.

Great Revival

In Stage Five - Battlefield Strategies – Fear/Anxiety, a reference was made to the Book of Revelation, in which John describes the Second Coming.[139] In his book, he writes that the final battle of good versus evil, also called Armageddon,[140] will lead to a conclusive outcome. There will be signs pointing to this battle which will commence in the Jezreel Valley, Israel, on the base of Mt. Megiddo. The respective signs or prophecies will include a falling away from the church and a counterbalance called the Great Revival, where the gospel will be proclaimed.

Descendants of God's chosen people, the Israelites, whose ancestors were centuries earlier scattered to distant countries from the Promised Land,[141] will return to Israel. Wickedness will be rampant and consume most of the world's people. Natural disasters like hurricanes, typhoons, earthquakes, flooding, and wildfires will occur. There will be wars and rumors of wars while Babylon—Iran and Iraq---will fall, and Zion—Israel---will be restored.

While many Christian warriors will not fight in this final battle in Israel, many will be involved in skirmishes leading up to the final

---

[139] George Barna. *The Second Coming of The Church* (Nashville: Thomas Nelson, Inc., 1998), Preface.

[140] Charles C. Torrey, "Armageddon," *Harvard Theological Review* 31, no. 3 (1938): 237-248.

[141] Nili Wazana. *All the Boundaries of the Land: The Promised Land in Biblical Thought in Light of the Ancient Near East.* (University Park: Penn State Press, 2013), 185.

battle. While Revelation is highly debatable, many believe this is a crucial tenet at the end times. Pastors must be aware that they live in a world that does not like Christians. These are the warriors this document is intended to address.

In the last days, there will be self-proclaimed spokespeople of the gospel who will preach false doctrines, and some will claim to be the Messiah. The battle lines between good and evil will never be more clearly defined for wise people who can see the spiritual truth. However, for the spiritually blind, the connection to this fact will be blurrier than ever. Many self-proclaimed ministers of the gospel will undermine the effectiveness of good pastors proclaiming the Gospel of Jesus Christ. As Sun Tzu writes in *The Art of War*, "Keep your friends close, and your enemies closer."[142]

The challenge for the Christian soldier will be to expose evil's deception and bring clarity between the opposing forces. In many ways, the battle will be fought in gray areas between light and darkness. These areas are identified by a morsel of truth, making the fact believable yet fraught with apostasy. Today, we already witness the power and persuasion of evil, which has corrupted many believers and closed their eyes to the gospel's truth. The world, the flesh, and the devil will be overwhelming except for God's power. Focusing on Christ and the cross will be paramount in this age.

Cost of War

In his classic The Cost of Discipleship, Dietrick Bonhoeffer, arguably the most renowned theologian of the twentieth century, described that adherence to the gospel is crucial for our salvation and victory in battle. Culture has always influenced the church, but it seems to have accelerated over the past few decades. Living a Christian life will not be easy because we live in an imperfect world, and since

---

[142] Christopher Scanlon and John Adlam. ""Keep your friends close, and your enemies closer". Sun-tzu, Chinese military strategist (~ 400 BC) [1] This chapter is based on and adapted from a longer paper published in the journal *Organizational and Social Dynamics*, vol. 11 (2). pp. 175-195, under the title 'Who watches the watchers? Observing the dangerous liaisons."

we attempt to live by a godly standard, we become enemies of the state. The Voice of the Martyrs[143] tracks numbers that show more Christian missionaries are martyred today than when statisticians began keeping track over one hundred years ago.

Early church history and Christian Martyrs – NOW[144] show that 65% of Christians have been killed because of their faith between 1900 and 2000. According to a missionary to China and pastor in the Anglican Church of South Carolina, Christian persecution is coming to America and, in some ways, is already here. This confirms the words of Jesus in Luke 9:22, "The Son of Man must suffer many things, and be rejected by the elders and chief priests and scribes, and be killed, and be raised the third day." If we, like Dietrich Bonhoeffer, take up our cross and follow Him, we will face the same suffering and rejection, and some will be killed for our faith in Jesus Christ.

Utopia

What was once taboo in the church has become mainstream, but much of the anything-goes culture has been codified into law. For instance, finding laws initially written according to Judeo-Christian[145] values would be a difficult assignment. The Supreme Court has overruled many religious standards, replaced them, or bridled them with entitlement laws. Examples include school prayer, corporal punishment, and the pledge of allegiance. These changes have had far-reaching effects on every segment of American society, including legal, military, education, medical, religious, and government.

Humanity has tried at various degrees of success to create a utopia[146] but often has failed because man cannot out-righteous God

---

[143] The Voice of the Martyrs. https://www.persecution.com.
[144] Christian Martyrs NOW. https://earlychurchhistory.org/martyrs/christian-martyrs-now/
[145] Mark Silk, "Notes on the Judeo-Christian Tradition in America," *American Quarterly*, 36(1). 65-85.
[146] Ruth Levitas, "For Utopia: The (Limits Of the) Utopian Function in Late Capitalist Society." *Critical Review of International Social and Political Philosophy* 3, no. 2-3 (2000): 25-43.

at the end of the day. For instance, President Lyndon Johnson's war on poverty is an example of man's attempt to out-righteous God, but we know this program failed miserably. It began in the early 1960s and cost hundreds of millions from the nation's treasury. Yet, poverty and hunger can still exist in the world's most prosperous countries.

FALSE MESSIAHS

Numerous attempts to create a socialist[147] society for equality, whether through experiments with communal life in a kibbutz,[148] have failed or been modified. Proponents of socialism desire to level the playing field through political extremes like Nazism or Communism. Many narcissistic psychopaths leading apocalyptic cults offering religious freedom, like Charles Manson and his family, Jim Jones, the People's Temple, or David Koresh and the Branch Davidian, have also failed. In their wake, many blind followers were led to their deaths. Society is full of imposters of the world's true light, Jesus Christ. The only way to a perfect world is through the narrow gates of heaven by God's only Son.

Armageddon will include an Apocalyptic period where the Four Horsemen[149] of conquest, war, famine, and death will be unleashed on the world. Ezekiel lists these devastations as the sword, famine, wild beasts, and pestilence or plague. Paul writes in 2 Timothy 3:1-4:2: "Know that in the last days, perilous times will come...but you must continue in the things you have learned and been assured of... the Holy Scriptures...preach the word! Be ready in season and out of season." This confirms the need for a Battle Plan for victory over evil.

After all the preparations for war are completed, the implementation of the Battle Plan begins. We learn from the Bible that our fight is for the hearts and minds of humanity. We learn from

---

[147] Janos Kornai. *Contradictions and Dilemmas: Studies on the Socialist Economy and Society*. (Cambridge: MIT Press. 1986), Preface.
[148] Yonia Talmon. *Family and Community in the Kibbutz,* Vol. 67 (Cambridge: Harvard University Press, 1972), 143.
[149] Slavoj Zizek. *Living in the End Times* (Brooklyn: Verso Books. 2011), 48.

the Old Testament that the mission is God's, not ours. We know victory is complete if we follow God's will and obey His commands.

Faith Restored

Field manuals[150] discuss field hospitals for the care of the soldier. A spiritual soldier's mental health and well-being are necessary to keep the army of God ready to engage in battle. This objective is fulfilled with clergy care centers or retreats where help is provided for the wounded spiritual warriors. They can rest, refresh their souls, and gain strength to return to the battlefield. This final battle will not convene or conclude easily; it has already begun and will be ever-increasing for years. Hostile actions will not cease until the last shell is fired and good has overcome evil.

Finally, logistics will coordinate with the field hospitals, which are essential to the battle rhythm[151] and the final battle plan. This objective is met by keeping the troops spiritually well-fed. Regular Bible study, prayer, daily devotions, meditation, and exercise are the meals where the soldiers are refreshed with the nutrition needed to be fit for battle. A steady diet of worship music and hymns while viewing God's glory through religious art and professional counseling is necessary to keep the soldier's spirits connected to his calling. These ingredients will refresh, renew, and restore the spiritual warrior and prepare him to fight another day.

Stage Seven – Battle for Victory – Hope/Peace

Finally, the seventh theater concludes the Seven Stage Reset. Hope is in the name of Jesus Christ. This step is also considered

---

[150] John A. Nagi, James F. Amos, Sarah Sewall, and David H. Petraeus. *The US Army/ Marine Corps Counterinsurgency Field Manual* (Chicago: University of Chicago Press, 2009), Introduction.

[151] Lorraine Duffy, Alex Bordetsky, Eric Bach, Ryan Blazevich, and Carl Oros. *A Model of Tactical Battle Rhythm* (San Diego: Space and Naval Warfare Systems Command, 2004.) PowerPoint Presentation.

a battle because clergies must continue to 'Fight the good fight.'[152] Pastors will repeatedly fall if they think they have arrived and there is no more work to be accomplished. A pastor's faith and trust must be replenished through regular worship, Bible study, and prayer. The reset begins with repentance, love, and forgiveness.

We know that Jesus counts forgiveness as the cornerstone of renewal and restoration and sternly warns everyone: "For if you forgive men their trespasses, your heavenly Father will also forgive you. But if you do not forgive men their trespasses, neither will your father forgive them."[153] These avenues will lead to increased hope and a "peace that passes all understanding."[154]

In Larry Richards's *The Full Armor of God,* we learn that Roman soldiers were fitted with special footgear.

> Now, Paul turns to another subject, peace, which he develops in Ephesians (2:11-4:16). The equipment he selects as his mnemonic device is a pair of military sandals worn by Roman legionnaires. Paul reminds us that we are to advance with our feet fitted with the readiness that comes from the gospel of peace . . . Let the peace of Christ rule in your hearts since you were called to peace as members of one body. And be thankful... It is a beautiful and calming picture. Oh, there are tensions. The phrase bear with each other means "put up with." And the fact that there is a need for forgiveness makes it clear that people still say and do things that hurt. Yet, through it all, God's people know an inner peace that enables them to be compassionate, kind, and patient. And through it all, peace finds expression in the love that binds them together in

---

[152] 2 Tim.4:7.
[153] Matt. 6:14-15.
[154] Phil. 4:6.

perfect unity. This is the life of leisure to which God calls you and me.[155]

Nevertheless, Paul reminds us to guard ourselves with the Armor of God primarily because he gave the final charge to Timothy, saying, "In fact, everyone who wants to live a godly life in Christ Jesus will be persecuted, while evildoers and imposters will go from bad to worse, deceiving and being deceived."[156]

Chapter four will discuss proposed retreats and comparisons. It will include preventative therapies and solutions and a look back from clergies who have weathered the storm, so to speak, and survived to engage in the battle for the lost for another day.

---

[155] Larry Richards. *Full Armor of God: Sandals of Peace* (Grand Rapids: Baker Books. 2013), 71.
[156] 2 Tim. 4:12-13.

CHAPTER FOUR

Proposed Clergy Care Retreat

Comparisons

German composer George Frideric Handel creates in his famous composition Messiah,[157] the majestic Worthy *of the Lamb that Was Slain,* wherein the lyrics tell of Jesus Christ, who redeemed the world by his blood on the cross at Golgotha[158]. This highlights the theological and spiritual foundation of the Slains Retreat and is the theme of this ministry. The desired outcome of Slains Ministries is not as much a solution as it is a reset to retrieve the pastor, priest, or preacher before they fall off the proverbial cliff. Reclamation and recovery are tools that allow clergies to be made whole again.

A central source for clerics leaving their ministries can be traced to burnout. Mayo Clinic describes burnout as "a state of physical or emotional exhaustion that also involves a sense of reduced

---

[157] George Frideric Handel, Alfred Mann, and Charles Jennens. *Messiah* (Rutgers University Documents of Music and Continuo Music Press, In., 1989).

[158] Joan E. Taylor, "Golgotha: A Reconsideration of the Evidence for the Sites of Jesus' Crucifixion and Burial," *New Testament Studies* 44, no 2 (1998): 180-203.

accomplishment and loss of personal identity."[159] Kyle Rhone writes in *Christianity Today*:

> But a more sinister risk accompanies burnout: "Burnout makes a pastor vulnerable to all kinds of ethical and moral failure," Rivers said. "The more emotionally exhausted you are, the more vulnerable you become to choices you would not make at healthier times and in a healthier frame of mind... "A lot of the moral failures and spiritual abuse we're seeing in the church right now have some foundation in the culture that pastors are working in," he said. Burnout is like a pressure cooker. The tension slowly builds, and without some release valve, the temperature of discouragement becomes unbearable. In his *Atlantic* article, Derek Thompson wrote, "Strange as it sounds, the increase in self-reported burnout is happening in industries where workers are less likely to quit. And pastoral ministry isn't a vocation that people often quit. The reasons for this are many and complex. "Few vocations are as deeply vocational as pastoral ministry," said Ward at Denver Seminary. "There's this deep sense of calling by God and to the people of God. It's not something you shake off and go into insurance." Pastors might stay too long for numerous reasons: a sense of obligation, unhealthy ownership, or misunderstood duty to God. Financial struggles can also keep the exit locked as pastors approach retirement.[160]

---

[159] Mayo Clinic. https://www.mayoclinic.org/burnout.
[160] Kyle Rohane, *Christianity Today*. May/June 2022. ChristianityToday.com. Page 49.

"The Cleveland Clinic discusses this as a mental health problem in an article entitled "What is Burnout?"[161] They identify five signs to look for in burnout. These signs are 1) Fatigue, 2) Apathy, 3) Headaches, 4) Diet, and 5) Sleep patterns.

One of the foremost objectives of Slains Clergy Care Retreat will be to nurture the wounded pastor. The retreat will provide pastors with personal time and collective space to resonate with fellow pastors, sharing each other's sense of calling and purpose. Part and parcel of this objective will be the aim to help pastors see more clearly their ministries and their ministry habits. Prudent counseling will help pastors learn to adapt to areas where there is room to grow and flourish first as a person and then as a clergy member.

The most crucial starting point in this healing ministry is for the participant to see the brokenness all ministers share. Christian pastors from every denomination must be honest about themselves as sinners who, like everyone, need occasional help. It is easy for pastors to fall victim to the adoration and praise the world showers on them. Clerics are often placed on a pedestal like a judge, a politician, or a medical doctor. The adoring crowds can lead a pastor to a false impression of his value and importance, often leading to a God-like persona. A pastor must never become a victim of these songs of praise and remember that the praise belongs to God.

Plan of Action

Slains Ministries is being established as a clergy care retreat requiring a team of professionals to provide care and comfort for the clergy participants who have been wounded after years of serving on the front lines. Thus, there are three main components to its success. The first is a vision. The second is developing a strategic plan followed by a plan of action. The third is a marketing plan established

---

[161] What Is Burnout? –Here's How to Deal with Feeling Physically and Emotionally Tired. Cleveland Clinic. Health Essentials. https://health.clevelandclinic.org/signs-of-burnout/

to recruit participants. These three elements will lead to a successful enterprise.

The first phase was to identify the need. The solution was a vision for a Clergy Care Center to help prevent wounded pastors from leaving the ministry as they have in record numbers. It was necessary to gather research on the method and scope of a Clergy Care Center, otherwise known as a strategic plan. Once the framework was established, legal documents were requested to be crafted to formalize a healing center for wounded clergy. Included in these documents were Articles of Incorporation and a Not-for-Profit assignment through the S.C. Secretary of State.

A marketing and fundraising team will need to be developed to request funding for an all-expense paid three-day retreat. Staff members will need to know how to write grants for access to public grants. An executive director and support staff who can organize staff and manage an office will need to be recruited. A board of directors from various professions must guide the executive director's efforts and spearhead the fundraising operations. A treasurer is needed to keep the books in order. A Certified Public Accountant is necessary to help navigate the ins and outs of public accountability in the Internal Revenue Service.

The second phase includes recruiting trained professionals who have expert knowledge of areas such as addictions and recovery. Music therapy, Art therapy, and Family Counseling are the three foundational pillars of the three-day retreat. Curricula in the various music and art disciplines will need to be developed. Treatment plans are a necessary component of providing excellent counseling care.

The third phase will include a scout team to search for a place to rent, buy or build as a retreat center for the incorporated name determined to be Slains Ministries. Once a destination for the center is established, the healing process under Slains can begin in earnest. It will not be easy, but every good thing starts with a vision of a better world. An overriding theme is that the Slains Ministry Care Center must be quartered near the ocean, the mountains, or a lake. The general public sees these places as places of rest and have become intertwined in the psyche. Therefore, the scout team will seek a respite place at or near these locations. Ultimately, God will guide this ministry to where the most benefit for clergy can occur.

Retreat Proposal

Jesus often escaped into the wilderness to pray and meditate with his Father to regain strength.[162] So, by his example, Christians, primarily clergy, need to find a place of respite to regain their strength. Slains Ministry hopes to provide this place of peace—a place to pray, meditate, and renew strength in body, mind, and spirit.

A three-day retreat is proposed to refresh, restore, and renew the broken spirits of the clergy. It is hoped this will slow the exit of pastors and keep them in the good fight, as Paul described. This study utilized several observation elements, including personal interviews, on-site visitations, and a questionnaire, to develop a working model.

This book has been more ecological since it took place outside of the confines of a church. Many trips to similar recovery and healing sanctuaries provided a hands-on analysis of what may be the best treatment plans for Slains Retreat. Internet research and telephone interviews were utilized to fill the void from the hands-on inspections and one-on-one interviews with retreat staff. While there was no mirror image of what Slains Retreat will ultimately become, there were compelling administrative, staffing, and treatment plans and suggestions that will combine to provide an exemplary model for treating wounded pastors. Almost every retreat researched had something good to offer.

The American Anglican Council (AAC)[163] spearheads a clergy care program that prevents clergy burnout in Loganville, Georgia. This organization is involved in many other areas of clergy health and well-being. They have years of experience in the treatment and

---

[162] Mark 6:46.
[163] "Clergy Care and Wellness," Anglican American Council, accessed September 7, 2021, https://americananglican.org/project/for-clergy/.

recovery area yet perform most of their treatment through seminars and internet meetings on Zoom[164] rather than in a retreat setting.

One of the most effective programs offered by the AAC falls under the Daniel Leadership Institute. This Institute is led by the Rev. Canon Phillip J. Ashley, President and CEO, and the Rev. Canon Mark Eldredge, Director of Anglican Revitalization Ministries. It is multi-layered and focuses on the laity, corporate support, and therapy plans. Their Clergy Care Group is the vehicle that most supports clergy needs. Under this group, the clergy is formed into teams to focus on "praying for each other, growing in Christlikeness together, and holding each other mutually accountable."[165] The four care areas and descriptions from the website are:

> Accountability – Clergy often feel they need to hide the actual state of their heart and soul. Clergy Care Groups are places to be vulnerable, honest, and trusting in others who can help carry struggles and provide accountability. For implementing spiritual disciplines, addressing family matters, or battling temptations, fellow group members become accountability partners.
>
> Support – A primary rule in these groups is that members do not try to fix one another. Instead, groups are where each person can practice being a listening ear and a voice of support rather than giving advice. It is also a comforting realization that many challenges are common to all. Instead of letting these problems create isolation, clergy care groups allow members to share their burdens and lift their spirits.

---

[164] Jeremy N. Bailenson, Department of Communication, Stanford University "Nonverbal overload: A theoretical argument for the causes of Zoom fatigue." (2021).

[165] Daniel Leadership Institute, The Rev. Canon J. Phillip Ashley, President and CEO. https://americananglican.org?daniel-leadership-institute/.

Prayer – Many people ask clergy to pray for them, but few know how to pray for clergy. Since Clergy Care Groups allow members to be vulnerable and honest, each member knows how to pray for others in a private and safe setting.

Friendship – Genuine friendship is rare among the clergy, who are usually uncomfortable building friendships with parishioners. CCG members become friends through the shared journey of spiritual disciplines, bearing one another's burdens, praying for one another, and fellowshipping together each week.

The Daniel Leadership Institute also provides a separate Clergy Spouse Care Group that satisfies clergy spouses' unique demands.

The Barnabas Horse Foundation (BHF) is in Myrtle Beach, S.C. but has horse stables in Murrells Inlet, S.C. It is a 501 c (3) non-profit corporation and has been in operation since 2011. It was founded by Sue McKinney, executive director, who has publicly identified herself as a victim of abuse. BHF assists victims of sexual assault, child abuse, bullying, domestic violence, and human trafficking. This program is unique and inspiring because it incorporates animals, specifically horses, in the healing process and treats victims of all ages. Clergies are not considered victims per se, as are the target groups of BHF, but they can relate to similar symptoms of stress, depression, and burnout. Programs like this use proven methods of animal therapy that Slains Ministries can adapt.

BHF has expanded its equine therapies to special needs and veterans in a safe and secure environment. They also include first responders who work on the front lines to protect the public. These responders share the same challenges of grief and trauma that can develop into post-traumatic stress and other disorders at greater levels. Many counselors of PTSD who are involved with veterans or first responder personnel trace the same symptoms. Thus, considering the spiritual warrior, these shared therapies are helpful for the wounded clergies. Workshops that include physical, emotional, cognitive, and relationship therapies are a gateway to a solution and reset. BHF therapies are proprietary.

The Big Red Barn Retreat (BRBR) in Blythewood, S.C., offers healing treatment through the Warrior PATHH and Struggle Well Programs. They are located on a multi-acre compound outside the Ft. Jackson U.S. Army Training Facility and are designated as a 501 c (3) nonprofit that provides a non-traditional wellness program. Also, BRBR provides professional counseling and interactive programs that help active-duty and veteran military warriors, first responders, and their immediate families. Participants begin with a seven-day retreat on-site that continues for another year or more if needed.

They offer residential and non-residential accommodations for those participating in their programs. The cornerstone treatment of the Warrior PATHH program focuses on the use of Transcendental Meditation (TM). BRBR expects that an afflicted, wounded, active-duty, veteran or first responder can reach positive mental wellness through TM. BRBR treats PTSD, stress, anxiety, and depression with reasonable success. Their treatment and counseling therapies are proprietary. This facility provides expertise in administering multi-day treatment plans and information about stress, anxiety, and depression that benefit Slains Ministries. This is helpful since pastors experience these symptoms from burnout. BRBR believes their treatment is transformative.

The Billy Graham Training Center at the Cove[166] offers a three-day retreat in Asheville, N.C. They provide a choice of four retreats designed for the pastor and spouse to rest, rejuvenate, relax, and restore one's soul. The typical retreat begins with the arrival, dinner, first session, and then fellowship. The next full day begins with breakfast, morning seminar, lunch, quiet time, dinner, and evening

---

[166] "Billy Graham Training Center at the Cove," Billy Graham Evangelistic Association," accessed November 5, 2021, About (billygraham.org).

seminar. The third day begins with breakfast, a morning seminar, and departure before lunch. The Billy Graham Training Center provides lodging and meals, including seminars, ranging from $25.00 per person to $50.00 per couple. The Cove serves various interest groups, from the military to Spanish-speaking participants. From their website are listed the following programs:

> COVE PROGRAMS offers life-changing Bible teaching, soul-stirring worship, and the fellowship of those who hunger to know God more deeply. Seminars vary in length, but most begin with afternoon registration, a delicious buffet dinner, an evening session on the first day, and conclude late morning on the final day.
>
> AN EVENING AT THE COVE and CHRISTMAS AT THE COVE features a concert by a famous Christian artist and a savory buffet dinner prepared by our chefs. Youths age nine and up may participate.
>
> INTENSIVE BIBLE TRAINING consists of seminars designed for anyone who wants to take an in-depth approach to understanding a specific topic or section of the Bible. They feature seminary-level instructors.
>
> MEN'S RETREAT is a program for men and boys ages 15 and up. It features inspirational messages and uplifting music.
>
> MILITARY RETREATS are programs that include free materials, meals, and lodging for active-duty, Guard, and Reserve military members and their spouses. Participants study

Scripture with practical applications for the unique experiences of military life.

PASTOR RENEWAL RETREATS. These programs include free meals and on-property lodging for one actively serving senior pastor and spouse per church and one associate pastor and spouse per year. Each retreat provides the opportunity to interact with peers and receive insight and instruction from experienced Christian leaders. A minimal materials fee is required ($30).

SEMINARIO EN ESPANOL (SEMINAR IN SPANISH). Este seminario será presentado totalmente en español con el objetivo de animar y fortalecer a los creyentes de habla hispana. This seminar is presented entirely in Spanish, to encourage and strengthen Hispanic believers.

SENIOR ADULT EVENTS. These programs, open to individuals and church groups, are designed for people ages 55 and up.

WOMEN'S EVENTS. These events are designed for women and girls ages 15 and up. They feature inspirational messages and uplifting music.

BUILD YOUR OWN COVE EXPERIENCE. You can customize your time away from God and build your Cove experience. Combine an inspiring seminar with a Come Early or Stay

Over opportunity, an adjacent seminar, a Personal Spiritual Retreat, or An Evening at The Cove.[167]

The Retreat at Wooden Creek is a new clergy care center on Johns Island, South Carolina. It is sponsored by Seacoast Church, a coastal assembly with a membership of 14,000 spread over thirteen campuses. It has links to over one thousand churches that are part of a worship assembly in North America and encompasses everywhere from the East to the West Coast. It is the vision of Rev. Greg Surratt.

These churches provide a constant flow of pastors available to attend the retreat for several days of respite. Most of these pastors stay in a large two-story structure that was initially a private family residence. It can accommodate as many as 20 weekly guests. It sits on 14 acres, conveniently bordering the marshlands. An additional 25 acres are available, if needed, but are not a part of the designated retreat. The property has a large pier on the waterway for boating and saltwater fishing. The residence provides a large kitchen and tables to accommodate several guests.

There are evening worship meeting rooms that begin after dinner and last until 9:00 p.m. There are walking nature trails and a five-acre pond for freshwater fishing. In the basement is a gym for daily exercise. The days are designed for self-motivated meditation, music, art, exercise, and personal reflection. The only organized treatment or counseling is the nightly Bible study. It is a form of group therapy.

Ministering to Ministers (MTM) is a Virginia-based clergy care center. Their motto is help, hope, and renewal for ministers in crisis. This ministry is similar to the objectives of the Slains Ministry. The following narrative is found on the website of MTM.

---

[167] https://static.billygraham.org/sites/thecove.org/uploads/prod/2023/01/14354-Cove-2023-Program-Guide-Web-Download.

Rev. Dr. Donald R. Hayes, DTh DMin

THE HISTORY OF MINISTERING TO MINISTERS[168]

In 1994, a group of ministers who'd gone through forced termination and interested laypeople joined to form Ministering to Ministers as a non-profit foundation to serve clergy in crisis. Ministering to Ministers offers HOPE for ministers and their families in all faith groups who are experiencing challenging employment-related situations through intervention and renewal; the Ministry offers HELP, HOPE, HEALING, AND RENEWAL through health and wellness promotion, including counsel, prayer, and support.

The centerpiece of our ministry is the 4–5-day Healthy Transitions Wellness Retreats for Ministers and Spouses. Through your donations, we can offer scholarships to all who attend so no one is left out. In June 2020, we will begin a series of workshops focusing on prevention topics to help keep ministers emotionally, spiritually, physically, and financially healthy.

Ministering to Ministers offers spiritual and emotional support, encourages good physical health to speed recovery from emotional and spiritual trauma, and helps clergy identify and clarify marketable, transferable work skills which can help lead to temporary employment.

The Ministry is a non-denominational organization financed through gifts from

---
[168] Ministering to Ministers. https://ministeringtoministers.org/.

The Battlefield of Faith

individuals, businesses, churches, denominations, and foundations and is strengthened by your prayers.

<u>Soul Shepherding Institute</u> is a for-profit treatment center directed by psychotherapists and ministers, Drs. Bill and Kristi Gaultiere provide spiritual care at their Soul Shepherding Institute[169] in Southern California, Northern California, Colorado Springs, Colorado, and Georgia. The following is from their website:

> Life-changing community and learning in four, 5-day retreats.
> Designed for pastors, spiritual directors, coaches, missionaries, ministry spouses, and other leaders, the Soul Shepherding Institute is a joyfully hospitable and Christ-centered learning community led by Bill and Kristi Gaultiere:
>
> - Doctor of Psychology, spiritual directors, and authors
> - Personally mentored by Dallas and Jane Willard
> - 25-year history of coaching and mentoring pastors and leaders
>
> Each retreat features:
>
> - Dynamic teaching on spiritual and emotional health
> - Guided experiences in Scripture meditation and prayer
> - Spiritual direction groups
> - Conversations with friends

---

[169] "Soul Shepherding Institute," Soul Shepherding, accessed November 6, 2021, <u>https://www.soulshepherding.org/institute/</u>.

- Opportunity for individual spiritual direction sessions
- Rest and solitude in beautiful places to help you hear God's voice

Their program offers four retreats, including proprietary sources for the following:

Spiritual Formation

The way to overcome stress, hurt, and sin is not "believe and do what's right" through apprenticeship to Jesus in his easy yoke. Learn the model and tools for growing in Jesus' rhythms of grace to cultivate intimacy with God, emotional and relational health, and fruitful ministry.

Soul Care Ministry

Our distinctive Christ-centered psychology sheds light on the stress and struggles that can defeat life with God. Learn how to use our unique Soul Shepherding tools for personal growth and ministry to others in spiritual direction, small groups, teaching, and church ministry.

Spiritual & Psychological Development

The spiritual life is not one-size-fits-all. Each stage in the journey needs different teaching, ministry, and disciplines. Our unique LIFE in CHRIST spiritual and emotional growth model provides customized coaching for you and the people you shepherd to thrive with Jesus.

Relationally Healthy Leadership

When we minister or lead out of ego, self-reliance, or hurry, it depletes our souls and hurts the people we love. The most effective leadership and ministry follow the way of Jesus—it's loving, relaxed, joyful, empowered, and effective. Learn critical practices to help you lead a healthy soul.

The cost of their programs ranges from a four-day retreat for $900.00 to $1,100.00 For a five-day retreat. A specially tailored retreat is available for $400.00 Per hour or $2000.00 daily.

The American Anglican Council (AAC) is under the leadership of the Anglican Church in North America (ACNA) and is led by the Most Rev. Foley Beach. It provides preventative care and solutions through its Clergy Care Groups and Soul Care Retreats through its Matthew 25 Initiative. Both groups help all interested participants but are not limited to clergy. Christine Warner is its executive director. Soul Care Retreat is an ongoing ministry under the Matthew 25 Initiative, as indicated in the following announcement and invitation to the November 13-14, 2019, gathering:

M25 Gathering & Soul Care Retreat

NOV 13, 2019 @ 10:00 AM - NOV 14, 2019 @ 1:00 PM CST

We are charged with bringing the light of Christ to the broken and dark places of the world, encountering Jesus in places of pain, and seeking healing. For centuries, Anglicans worldwide have been people of *"gardens and... springs... repairers of broken walls and restorers of community" (Isaiah 58) for all Anglicans in the ACNA*—a two-day virtual event featuring speakers, panel discussions, and a soul care retreat. Join us as we cast vision, share burdens, and spur on hope as we contend for Shalom.

As mentioned above, Soul Care Retreat is an ongoing ministry of the ACNA.

Another gathering met on July 30, 2021, for an Online Workshop via Zoom. The following issues were addressed in three segments: 11 am-12 pm CDT Biblical Spirituality, Brain Science, and Trauma.12 pm-1 pm CDT Contemplative Guided Prayer Exercises; 1 pm-2 pm CDT Soaking Prayer. These three segments are included in regular intervals for the treatment of clergy soul care. They are subjects that could be useful in the treatment plans for Slains Retreat.

Ministering to Ministers is active in Preventative Therapies and Solutions by organizing retreats in the Lynchburg, Va., and Birmingham, Ala., areas. Their webpage addresses the effects of ministry in the following article:

- Ministry is hard, and it remains one of the last occupations where such a vast array of functions is demanded and utterly dependent on relationships with volunteers and their productivity in changing environments.
- Southern California psychologist Richard Blackmon indicates "about 75% go through a period of stress so great that they consider quitting" (Dirmann, T. (1999, January 29). Pastoral pressures test faith; religion: Demands of spiritual leaders leave many suffering from 'pastor burnout.')
- Clergy often abuse themselves with unrealistic expectations, schedules, and deferred self-care. Ninety percent of pastors report working between 55 to 75 hours per week, which is hardly how to prepare for challenges and conflicts among persons in the church.
- Forty percent of pastors report serious conflict with a parishioner at least once a month. (Cited in Ministry

Missing Link, Statistics for Pastors, www.pastoralcareinc.com/statistics/).
- Forcibly terminated ministers are more likely to experience negative marital and family satisfaction, have higher levels of stress and more physical and emotional health problems, and consider leaving ministry – than other ministers (MN Tanner, AM Zvonkovic. (2011). Forced to leave, Pastoral Psychology.).
- Overall, clergy and their spouses scored high – and in some cases above the clinical cutoff on Generalized Anxiety Disorder (GAD) and Post-Traumatic Stress Disorder (PTSD). These couples also scored themselves as having experienced mobbing – bullying tactics – before the forced termination. (Tanner, Wherry and Zvonkovic, 2012)

Ministering to Ministers provides realistic counsel regarding the challenges of ministry, meaningful response, support in a crisis, and essential content for clergy training and continuing education in the hope of stable and durable ministries. They offer five retreats that address specific areas of concern as follows:

Emotional Wellness

- Telling Your Story
- Addressing Your Grief
- Increasing Your Self-Awareness
- Identifying, Understanding, and Managing Your Emotional Responses
- Listening to Spouses

Personal Wellness

- Thinking in Systems
- Resolving Disputes
- Understanding Affect Psychology
- Enhancing Your Emotional Intelligence

Physical Wellness

- Self-Care
- Unstructured Time

Spiritual Wellness

- Devotions
- Enriching Your Spiritual Self
- Praying for One Another

Call2Disciple was established to treat clergies with the following therapies before burnout. Erilynne Barnum founded this ministry, a continuing ministry led by The Rt. Rev. Thaddeus R. Barnum since her passing a few years ago. He is the chaplain and lead counselor in this organization. It is located on Pawley's Island, S.C. Bishop Barnum is a Bishop in Residence at All Saints Church, a member parish of the Diocese of the Carolinas and the Anglican Church in North America (ACNA). On their webpage is listed Soul Care for Pastors. Bishop John Miller gives his account of the need for healing for pastors in the following narrative:

> Shortly after retiring in July 2019, Bishop David Bryan and Bishop Thad, who oversee Call2Disciple, asked that I consider coming alongside them in the soul care ministry. Bishop Thad, who is on the frontline, was able to care for the increasing numbers of clergy seeking such assistance as they faced the endless demands of ordained leadership. After months of prayer, and with Archbishop Foley Beech's enthusiastic endorsement, I have accepted Thad's invitation to provide soul care to those pastors and priests within the Anglican Church of North America and beyond who are struggling to serve the Lord within the Body of Christ faithfully and fruitfully.

The Battlefield of Faith

Perhaps the most sobering fact about serving the Church as an ordained minister is that many clergies abandon their call long before retirement age, or they finish the race poorly. Pressures such as marital strife, family struggles, congregational expectations, and long hours addressing pastoral and administrative needs can leave a pastor weary and defeated. Sadly, the pastor often believes they have no safe person to turn to for help when that happens. Consequently, many pastors find themselves hopelessly isolated. Such aloneness renders them the perfect target for an attack by the Enemy, who specializes in neutralizing shepherds so that he can wreak havoc on the flock.

I envision the ministry of soul care to provide that "safe space" for pastors such that they experience the freedom to express transparently the problems they face and receive compassionate spiritual wisdom aligned with sound biblical principles. Accordingly, as a soul care provider, I function not as a mental health counselor psychoanalyzing problems or a ministry coach helping pastors to establish objectives and reach strategic goals. Instead, my role is to be a companion on the way, praying for and encouraging pastors while ever-redirecting their focus on Jesus—the unconditional lover of souls.[170]

Teresa Glenn provides counseling for female clergy and clergy wives and treatment as described in the call2disciple website:

---

[170] Call2Disciple. John Miller. https://www.call2disciple.com/john-miller.

Often clergy wives and female clergy are the sounding board, the listener, the one who prays for another, the one who gently asks questions to help someone look to Jesus. Yet, many clergy wives and female clergy do not have this 'person' to go to for themselves. "I don't have anyone I can talk to about this" is a common statement.

Two years ago, I joined the Call2Disciple team to offer Soul Care to clergy wives and female clergy. This ministry provides a safe place for these women to unload what burdens their hearts, to have a sounding board, and to have someone walk beside them confidentially, prayerfully, and steadfastly pointing them to Jesus.

Conversations cover a wide range of topics like the challenges of marriage, family life, other relationships, ministry, or a desire for discipleship. Video conversation is preferred (Facetime, Google Duo, Skype).[171]

Leader Care at the Southern Baptist Convention, led by Mr. Brooks Faulkner and Dr. Charles H. Chandler, is an excellent resource for preventative care, as well as *Ministering to Ministers Foundation*, an interdenominational mission led by The Rev. Dr. Bill Turner, pastor of South Main Baptist Church and *Central Congress of American Rabbis* led by Rabbi Matthew Michaels of Houston's Congregational Emanuel Synagogue.

These organizations have years of experience treating the needs of pastors who have approached a crossroads in their ministries. Eugene H. Peterson says in *Christianity Today*, "The soul is the essence of the human personality. The Cure of Souls is the Scripture-directed, prayer-shaped care devoted to persons singularly or in

---

[171] Call2Disciple. Teresa Glenn. https://www.call2disciple.com/teresa-glenn.

groups not to exceed five participants in sacred and profane settings. It is a determination to work at the center, to concentrate on the essentials."[172]

Therefore, a vigorous, refreshed, restored, and renewed spirit is a healthy soul that can serve the Lord more meaningfully and purposefully. In the context of ministry, clinical pastoral treatment reveals that the *recovery of the soul* is a critical component of the healing process. This phrase is used in CPE programs: "Clinical Pastoral Education (CPE) combines professional education and hands-on experience, providing spiritual care to patients, families, and staff members in multi-faith settings."[173] Helping find and restore a lost or injured soul is a ministry of the church. It is inherent in the salvation narrative. The healing ministry discussed here is designed for clergy of all denominations. This does not preclude the necessity of such a healing program for other professionals; instead, this program is designed specifically for ministers. The following news article covers a wide range of solutions for clergy care, including staffing needs:

> NASHVILLE, Tenn. (BP)–LeaderCare, a ministry to ministers and their families, sponsored by LifeWay Christian Resources of the Southern Baptist Convention, is expanding with added services and staff.
>
> Designed to provide personal development resources and crisis prevention, intervention, and restoration resources for pastors, staff members, and their families, LeaderCare began in May 1996, adding a 911-type crisis hotline.

---

[172] Eugene H. Peterson, "Curing Souls: The Forgotten Art," *Christianity Today*, accessed September 31, 2021, https://www.christianitytoday.com/pastors/1983/summer/8313048.html.

[173] Clinical Pastoral Education Program," Cedars Sinai, accessed October 5, 2021, https://www.cedars-sinai.org/patients-visitors/spiritual-care/clinical-pastoral-education.html.

Rev. Dr. Donald R. Hayes, DTh DMin

Joining the LeaderCare staff are Barney Self, hotline specialist; Dallas Speight, retreat specialist, and counselor; and Bob Sheffield, ministers' advocate specialist. Later this year, a ministers' wives' specialist will be added to the staff. Self, a licensed marital and family therapist, has been the clinical director of Christian Counseling Services in Nashville, Tenn. He was formerly in private practice in marriage, family, and individual pastoral counseling.

He will counsel pastors, staff, and their families who call the LeaderCare hotline and provide appropriate referrals and follow-up for those he counsels. Speight, a licensed mental health counselor, has been director of pastoral services for Baptist Hospital, Pensacola, Fla., since 1994. He oversees retreats for pastors, staff, and spouses and coordinates personal development and career assessment programs.

Sheffield, a Lifeway employee since 1985, has been a church consultant in deacon and pastoral ministries in the pastor-staff leadership department. He will work with deacons, church committees, and other church leaders in their relationships with ministers and their families and develop resources to help pastor and staff search committees.

Other LeaderCare staff include Brooks Faulkner, senior LeaderCare specialist in compassion fatigue, personal growth, and random violence; Norris Smith, a specialist in conflict management and mediation; and Tommy Yessick, wellness specialist.

The Battlefield of Faith

Neil Knierim, manager of the LeaderCare section, said the hotline (1-888-789-1911), a 24-hour-a-day service, receives approximately 3,000 calls annually. Needs range from having someone to listen and pray with them to referring them to a provider for intensive psychiatric care.

In May 1999, LeaderCare assumed responsibility for Wounded Heroes, now known as Wounded Ministers, a ministry to depressed and hurting ministers begun by Southern Baptist evangelist Freddie Gage.

Career assessments are provided in individual and group sessions. Approximately 85 people are provided individual assessments each year, along with four group assessment sessions totaling 215 people per year. Knierim said most sessions include both the spouse and the minister.

Weekend events for ministers and spouses who have experienced a forced termination are called "Agenda for Healing." LeaderCare conducts nine of these events each year, with 200 total participants. The weekends include group therapy and support sessions to help couples work through issues related to termination.

LeaderCare conducts Personal and Professional Growth Seminars each year. Participants examine their skills, affirm their call, analyze their personalities and giftedness, and consider their ministry goals. This intensive event is limited to six people for each event. Extensive follow-up is done with each participant to monitor progress.

Minister/Spouse Marriage Enrichment events are conducted eight times yearly. These two-day events deal with relationships within a ministry marriage. Typical subjects are intimacy, communication, and prioritizing relationships and responsibilities. Approximately 350 couples participate each year.

Conferences for ministers who need encouragement and support are offered in various locations. The average attendance for each event is 130 ministers. Staff from LeaderCare, LifeWay President James T. Draper Jr., and a minister who has been through a challenging experience speak at these events.

"We have more than 1,000 counselors available through our state convention network and 90 clergy care organizations through which we can get help for persons with severe needs. Annually, we refer 300 couples and individuals to these resources."

LeaderCare also conducts and sponsors five church conflict mediations annually. LeaderCare has trained more than 400 people to conduct church mediations. Approximately 40 mediations are done annually by state convention-related mediators.

This news article summarizes the various needs and treatments in the clergy care landscape. It is a desire that these treatment plans will be expanded one day to incorporate more areas of recovery and reset.

Slains Ministries

The vision for Slains Ministries is more attuned to The Billy Graham Training Center rather than the others, where participants can attend free of charge because the Slains Ministry Foundation will cover the cost of housing, meals, training, and counseling materials as well as pay salaries for staff help and certified counselors and specialists. Paying attention to the clergy or helping the helper will pay dividends for the future church. In many ways, the ministry is a minefield, and the clergy is often ill-prepared for the vocation.

Many churches have adopted business models versus mission models, which undermine the effectiveness of churches' ministry to the spiritual needs of its members. As mentioned, a part of this study may envision a new way to "Church" as we know it. Since it is clear that the ways of the world have invaded the ways of church life as we know it, we may want to reconsider exorcising the worldly ways for the ways of God.

Proposed Seminar

The three-day retreat will follow this preliminary schedule. Mondays and Fridays are travel days, so the retreat's core will be three days.

Monday – Arrive and sign in. Receive room assignment.

6:00 to 6:30 pm: Compline in the Chapel.
6:35 to 7:30 pm: Dinner in the Dining Hall.
7:35 to 9:00 pm: Reception until lights out.

Tuesday – 7:00 to 7:30 am: Morning Prayer in the Chapel.

7:35 to 8:30 am: Breakfast in the Dining Hall.
9:00 am to 10:30 am: First Session (Part 1) in Parish Hall.

Topic: This session will address the loss of the pastoral dream.[174]

    10:35 to 10:45 am: Morning Break.
    10:50 to 12:00 pm: First Session (Part 2).
    12:05 to 12:30 pm: Noon Day Prayer in Chapel.
    12:35 to 1:25 pm: Lunch in Dining Hall.
    1:30 to 3:25 pm: Second Session (Part 1) in Parish Hall.

Topic: This is a discussion on reconnecting to the pastoral dream.

    3:30 to 3:40 pm: Afternoon Break.
    3:45 to 6:00 pm: Second Session (Part 2).
    6:05 to 6:30 pm: Compline in Chapel.
    6:35 to 7:25 pm: Dinner in the Dining Hall.
    7:30 to 9:00 pm: Round Robin (Individual Counseling).

Wednesday – 7:00 am to 7:30 am: Morning Prayer in the Chapel.

    7:35 to 8:30 am: Breakfast in Dining Hall.
    9:00 am to 10:25 am: Third Session (Part 1) in Parish Hall.

Topic: This session will look at contemporary challenges in the church.

    10:30 to 10:40 am: Morning Break.
    10:45 to 12:00 pm: Third Session (Part 2) in Parish Hall.
    12:05 to 12:30 pm: Noon Day Prayer in Chapel.
    12:35 to 1:30 pm: Lunch in Dining Hall.
    1:35 to 3:30 pm: Fourth Session (Part 1) in Parish Hall.

---

[174] Kurtes D. Quesinberry, "Accessing Post-Traumatic Stress Disorder Care as a Resource for Pastoral Grief Counseling," *TTGST Theological Journal*, 12.1 (2009): 90-102, 20124-246.pdf (ttgst.ac.kr).

The Battlefield of Faith

Topic: Where do we see ourselves moving forward?

    3:35 to 3:45 pm: Afternoon Break.
    3:50 to 6:00 pm: Fourth Session (Part 2) in Parish Hall.
    6:05 to 6:30 pm: Compline in Chapel.
    6:35 to 7:30 pm: Dinner in Dining Hall.
    7:30 to 9:00 pm: Round Robin (Individual Counseling).

Thursday – 7:00 to 7:30 am: Morning Prayer in the Chapel.

    7:35 to 8:30 am: Breakfast in the Dining Hall.
    9:00 am to 10:30 am: Fifth Session (Part 1) in Parish Hall.

Topic: How do we reengage our current or future ministry?

    10:35 to 10:45 am: Morning Break.
    10:50 to 12:00 pm: Fifth Session (Part 2).
    12:05 to 12:30 pm: Noon Day Prayer in Chapel.
    12:35 to 1:30 am: Lunch in Dining Hall.
    1:35 to 3:30 pm: Sixth Session (Part 1) in Parish Hall.

Thursday afternoon's session is optional for those who need to begin home early.

Topic: Where do we go from here?

    3:35 to 3:45 pm: Afternoon Break.
    3:50 to 6:00 pm: Sixth Session (Part 2).
    6:05 to 6:30 pm: Compline in Chapel.
    6:35 to 7:30 pm Dinner in Dining Hall.
    7:35 to 9:00 pm: Round Robin (Individual Counseling).

Friday - 7:00 to 7:30 am: Morning Prayer in Chapel.

    7:35 to 8:30 am: Breakfast in Dining Hall.

The topics mentioned above are initial considerations for the treatment of participants. These topics will be regularly amended to meet the needs of the clergies as determined from their application Questionnaire (See Appendix). Topics will sometimes be different in each session or retreat.

While developing this pilot program, the Slains Ministry team hopes each participant will be a testament to the effectiveness of this proposed retreat. It will be a success if their respective ministries have been reclaimed in relationship with God, their families, and their churches. Included in a master plan[175] will be a survey to gauge the effectiveness of Slains Ministries' future reset programs for improvement. Thus, the necessity for this pilot program.

Conclusion

The success of Slains Ministries will be provided in the proof of recovery or wholeness of the participant. A psychologist can only take a person to his cognitive/visceral level, but a trained theologian can take that person beyond himself into the presence of God. If Slains points the clergy toward the healing pathway, the wounded warrior will be on the road to recovery and become whole again. Thus, Slains will fulfill the words of Jesus, who proclaimed, 'I come that they may have life and that they may have it more abundantly.'[176]

---

[175] "Master plan," *Merriam Webster*, accessed September 23, 2022, https://www.merriam-webster.com/dictionary/master%20plan.

[176] John 10:10.

CHAPTER FIVE

Why A Clergy Care Center Matters

Life Experiences of Five Pastors

This chapter demonstrates the need for a Clergy Care Center. It is presented from the real-life experiences of five clerics who have, on their own, successfully navigated the challenges that regularly undermine the Christian ministry. They represent pastors who have not lost their joy for the vocation they were called to fulfill. This does not mean they did not struggle, but their commitment and determination kept them in the battle for the hearts, minds, and spirits of the faithful. The following tenet underscores the challenges clergies face in a world lorded over by the evil one.

We live in a secular world and are called to be witnesses to the gospel of Jesus Christ. Although we live in the world, Jesus calls us to be apart from the world. Jesus says, "I have given them Your word, and the world has hated them because they are not of the world, even as I am not of the world. I do not ask You to take them out of the world but to keep them from the evil one. They are not of the world, even as I am not of the world."[177] Humanity makes idols of

---

[177] John 17:14-16.

many things, including the government. If governments like China, Russia, or North Korea hate Christians, it is reasonable to state that believers are enemies of the state. Believers are often perceived as roadblocks that stand in the way of progress.

They are viewed this way because, as the Scripture says, "Although we live in the world, we are not part of it."[178] Christian values and standards are of a higher calling. Christians live by a set of commandments under the Lordship of Jesus Christ. Their allegiance is to their Heavenly Father and not the state. As Jesus proclaims in the Gospel of Mark, "Therefore render unto Caesar the things that are Caesars's and unto God the things that are God's."[179]

Modern Christians face the same challenges as those in the first century regarding righteous or unrighteous behavior. In many ways, life is a paradox that we must navigate daily. How do we live in the world and not be part of this world? This is the quandary for clergy to lead their congregations in God's ways rather than the world's. We either seek the things of this world, or we seek the things of God. The result is that they need to review their ministries regularly from top to bottom. They must rethink how the church is organized, communicates, relates to the gospel story, and connects meaningfully to people. As noted in *Faith for Exiles: 5 Ways for a New Generation to Follow Jesus in Digital Babylon:*

> The appeal of following Jesus jades most non-Christian youth and young adults. They reject organized religion, especially claims of an exclusive faith like Christianity. Many view the Bible as a book of oppression that is harmful to the minds of its devoted readers. Young Christians encounter condescension or downright hostility

---

[178] "How can believers be in the world, but not of this world?" GotQuestions, accessed September 02, 2022, https://www.gotquestions.org/in-but-not-of-world.html.
[179] Mark 12:17.

from their peers, instructors, and social elites in some influential places.[180]

If Christ is our example that we should turn the other cheek, then Christians are not expected to be oppressive in their behavior, but this virtue does not always hold. Christians lay claim to the gospel of a risen Lord and Savior, Jesus Christ. His message is to love God with all our hearts, souls, and minds and to love each other as Christ loved us. The distinction is that Christians live under Christ's leadership and abide by a moral standard of conduct that requires them to avoid the ways of this world.

The five clerics responded to a questionnaire on the Slains Ministries concept related to their spiritual journey. Their responses include segments of their testimonies. Their names and ecclesiastical endorsers are listed for validation but omitted in the results to protect their answers and encourage transparency. Their responses are interwoven in the answers.

This group addressed various therapies related to the treatment programs that could be most helpful for wounded clergy. They have in common the wounds of their respective ministries. They offer insight into other clergy facing similar burnout, rejection, and disinterest in their calling and describe how they recovered to reclaim their ministries. Their practical experience is invaluable.

Metaphorically speaking, individuals relate to Jesus more meaningfully by releasing their fears, anxieties, and depressions that bind them. One pastor stated that if they slay their inhibitions, they draw closer to Christ Jesus by nailing their sins to the proverbial cross. They leave their inhibitions behind and see the barriers to their ministry. Those barriers that were once roadblocks can become highways for restoration. Thus, they can connect to their calling and return to the battle for the hearts and minds of the believers they were called to lead. Slains Ministry seeks to help ministers decompress

---

[180] David Kinnaman and Mark Matlock, *Faith for Exiles: 5 Ways for a New Generation to Follow Jesus in Digital Babylon* (Grand Rapids: Baker Books, 2019), 27.

retained stresses and anxieties, thereby mitigating the pressures of ministry.

Slains Ministries will be designed along the tenets found in one of many books, including *Faith of Exiles* by David Kinnaman and Mark Matlock, who say, "The Babylon of the Bible is characterized as a culture set against the purposes of God—a human society that glories in pride, power, prestige, and pleasure."[181] In many ways, society parallels the days of Babylon. To describe this Babylon in the present age, Kinnaman and Matlock have coined the new phrase 'digital Babylon,' against which believers are waging an uphill battle.

Digital Babylon is represented by the computers, smartphones, tablets, televisions, smartwatches, and apps that seem to govern and direct our lives, limiting our choices between things of God and things of this world. Clerics face an uphill battle for the hearts and minds of believers. Thus, some churches have begun allowing digital media in worship services.

Interestingly, communication has been a challenge for clerics since the days of Christ. Many ministers have embraced these newfound ways of communication. By allowing and providing words to the songs sung projected on a wall or sending digital copies of their sermons to smartphones, the parishioner can sing the hymn or follow the sermon in real-time. This is a highly creative way of reaching out to the latest generation. Rather than bemoaning the use of technology, embracing it can be an advantage for the minister. This challenge provides an opportunity to rebuild the church under the biblical model used by previous generations.

However, today's church has allowed the culture to invade its sacred spaces in relationship to its theology and mission. The church has adopted a business model that is more secular than sacred. Decisions are made to provide and protect the institution—not to ensure salvation but to maintain the established order. Such a way of behavior has caused a great divide between small and large churches,

---

[181] Kinnaman and Matlock, *Faith for Exiles: 5 Ways for a New Generation to Follow Jesus in a Digital Babylon*, 23.

where most rural churches led by stand-alone pastors are fulfilling the church's mission, often selflessly serving the needy.

Many of these pastors are called tentmakers because they work full-time to receive a living wage while serving the church's needs without payment for services rendered. In contrast, large churches with adequate resources can provide a living wage for their pastor. This may be the breeding ground for clergy participating in the Slain's Ministry retreat. Wounded ministers from diverse backgrounds and conditions are invited to participate in this ministry. Here they can expect expert help in all areas that need spiritual care.

The church as we know it is changing. Some see it as a church without walls. Cardinal Avery Dulles points out six models of the church.[182] Timothy Keller says, "A center church theological vision (which) can empower all kinds of church models in all settings."[183] Recognizing this need for a central church vision, Slains Ministries leaves room for many healing programs, from individual to corporate. The vision of making a personal connection with God is the primary driver of this ministry.

God's agenda is to refresh, restore, and renew the Christian clergyman he has called into his service. Then the clergy will be reset and reclaimed. As Paul says in his epistle to the Romans, "Do not conform to the pattern of this world but be transformed by renewing your mind. Then you can test and approve what God's will is his good, pleasing, and perfect will."[184] In his epistle to the Ephesians, Paul says, "To be made new in the attitude of your minds, and to put on the new self, created to be like God in true righteousness and holiness."[185]

---

[182] Avery Cardinal Dulles, *Models of the Church* (New York: Random House, 2002). 181.
[183] Timothy Keller, *Center Church* (Grand Rapids: Zondervan, 2012), 25.
[184] Rom. 12:12.
[185] Eph. 4:23-24.

Seven Stage Reset Questionnaire

The following clergy agreed to participate in this questionnaire. They are as follows: Rev. Dr. Kurtes Quesinberry (Church of God of Prophecy), Rev. Kirby Winstead (Southern Baptist), Rev. Dr. Marshall Ivey (Presbyterian CUSA), Rev. Elgin Woodberry (Free Will Baptist), Rev. Samuel Tilden Boone (Church of Christ).

The Seven Stages of Reset, which have been created and developed to help wounded clergy, are as follows in sequential order:

1- Pride/Vanity................The Fall.
2- Doubt/Depression............The Consequence of Pride.
3- Temptation/Addiction.......The Consequence of Doubt.
4- Guilt/Despair..................The Consequence of Temptation.
5- Anxious/Fear..................The Consequence of Guilt.
6- Faith/Trust....................The Safety Net.
7- Hope/Peace/Joy..............The Reset with God.

These Seven Stages follow a sequence from the mountaintop into the valley, resetting into a restored relationship with God. The first stage is the fall. The following four stages are the results of the fall. The sixth stage is the safety net, while the seventh is the victory lap.

Part I: Preset – Starting point.

1. Do you believe the Christian church and ministry are in crisis? Y or N

    All five pastors answered yes.

2. Have you ever considered leaving your ministry for another vocation?   Y or N

    The pastors were split on this question. One said he is bi-vocational now, which could mean he would have left if he were a full-time pastor in a church in an economically challenged

The Battlefield of Faith

area that could not pay him a living wage. Another considered a new vocation but only in passing. He remained faithful to his calling, chalking it up as experience.

2a. If so, what were the circumstances?

> Of the answers that stood out, one mentioned the power brokers in the congregation who negotiated his discharge by misrepresenting him before the regional church leadership. In turn, he could not provide sufficient evidence to overturn the departure.

2b. What did you do to mitigate the circumstances?

> Again, this minister spent months in correspondence with his church hierarchy about the account above. Much to his chagrin, he was led along, seeming that his position had been predetermined without his chance to face his accusers. In every case, a consistent result was that each minister lost confidence in their hierarchy, leading to dismissal, inhibition, or license revoked.

2c. How did you overcome the challenges you faced?

> The above pastor could have left the ministry, but he valued his call to the ministry. Instead of leaving for a new vocation, he turned to other ministry avenues which were non-pastoral. He began work as a church worship leader, songwriter, street minister, home Bible study leader, and State Guard chaplain.

3. Could a ministry of healing help wounded ministers stay in service?   Y or N

All the pastors answered in the affirmative.

3a. What had the most profound effect on healing wounds you received in ministry?

Most pastors reported that their relationship with Jesus became the foundation of their recovery and present ministry. All of them stated that reinvesting in elements of ministry helped them reset their callings, such as working in food pantries and soup kitchens. Volunteerism kept them connected to their faith-based communities. Regular Bible studies and religious gatherings kept them engaged. All reported that their dependence on God and trust in him increased, and they had a more consistent and profound prayer life.

PART II: PRIDE/VANITY.

Proverbs 13:10 states that pride leads to a fall. The world advocates a quest for power, prestige, fame, and fortune.

4. Did pride play any part in your ministry wounding or decline? Y or N

    Not all the pastors agreed that pride played a role in their challenges or temporary times of being wounded.

    4a. If so, what happened? One said he had been nationally discredited, bringing him to a place of humility and discomfort. Another stated that he had been inhibited, which meant he was not authorized to perform specific sacramental duties that are part of his denominational tradition.

    4b. How were you reset? The first pastor began recovery by meeting with a new State Presbyter and beginning a path forward to redemption. He had to begin from the bottom and work his way upward again. The second pastor left his communion for another communion within his jurisdiction under a new bishop and hierarchy. In both cases, embarking on a new path, changing the scenery by moving to a new state and jurisdiction, or building from scratch was the beginning of resetting and restoring their woundedness.

4c. Did you receive help (professional or non-professional) to reset?

All the pastors closed ranks with their peers, but none reported having met with a professional counselor. Building or having a battle buddy or set of confidants who know you is vital to ministry. Having trusted friends who can be confided in is paramount to a pastor's mental, emotional, and spiritual well-being.

4d. Or, did you make the journey to reset on your own?

All reported that early challenges were met with self-help treatment, but as the challenges became more so, reaching out to a core group of confidants became more critical and necessary.

Part III. Doubt/Depression.

Left unabated, doubts can lead to depression. A protracted state of depression, if it becomes clinical, can lead to debilitation.

5. Did doubt visit you in your journey as a wounded clergy?
Y or N

Every pastor reported that doubt was a part of their journey. They went through bouts of depression or melancholy. They reached various levels of depression, some lasting short times, others lasting longer. Many reported a loss of appetite, energy, sleep, and general disinterest in life. Long walks in the woods, an increased focus on the positive rather than the negative, putting the past in the rearview mirror, quiet time, meditation, and calming music helped them begin their recovery.

5a. Were (or are) any lasting effects of doubt on your upward recovery?

All reported no lasting doubts unless being counted as strengthening them is an effect.

5b. What is the status of your journey toward healing (professional or personal)?

In both professional and personal life regarding healing, all the pastors reported that a more robust prayer life resulted from their ministry challenges.

5c. How did you navigate to a better place?

All reported that these were the ingredients to navigate to a better place through their prayer life and times of worship and meditation. Looking forward, not backward, was a significant turn of events on the path to reset. The pastors did not dwell on the past; putting their adverse circumstances in perspective was helpful. Looking at the larger picture helped them to focus more on their calling rather than themselves.

5d. List the steps you took, in chronological order, if you can.

All pastors began their road to recovery by being objective in their thoughts and actions. They analyzed their situation by reviewing the steps that began to unravel and developing a plan of action to regain their ministry. These actions included talking to family, looking for answers in Scripture, and finding the solutions to their problems in the Word of God.

Part IV. Temptation/Addiction.

The Bible states that we all face temptation, sometimes leading to addictions. Addiction knows no boundaries and can be almost anything. Consider addiction as 'idol worship' to help form your answers.

6. In your wounded state, did you develop any addictions? Y or N

    None of the pastors stated that they had turned to an addiction, whether it be alcohol, drugs, or tobacco. However, some had prior addictions which were no longer a part of their lives as ministers.

    6a. If yes, what can you tell us about it? Not applicable.

    6b. How did it affect your church, family, and ministry? Not applicable.

    6c. How did you recover from your addiction(s)? The one who reported a prior addiction stated that his break came with a miracle prayer. Now that he is a recovered addict, he has a greater testimony.

6d. Do you still struggle with addiction(s)? He no longer struggles with addiction.

Part V. Guilt/Despair.

Often, we review our history with heavy hearts and deep regrets. This is the essence of guilt and grief. Guilt or grief can lead to spiritual paralysis and ultimately affect ministries.

7. Have you dealt with grief regarding your wounding?   Y or N

The results from this question were mixed. Some did not experience grief, while others did have bouts of grief. One did not have grief but did deal with guilt. Another dealt with both grief and guilt. The pastor, who dealt only with guilt, felt he did not do all he could to repair his situation. One who dealt with grief and guilt reported that the simultaneous loss of their son compounded the loss of ministry. The shared grief, loss of ministry, and loss of a son were too difficult to separate at the emotional and psychological impact level. This situation illustrates that pastors are like everyone else. Their personal lives must be in conjunction with their vocational responsibilities as a shepherd, making ministry uniquely difficult.

7a. What instances did you face that led to your ministry-related grief?

Grief is very complex and difficult to articulate. For those who grieve over a broken ministry, it resembles losing a loved one, a lost job, a lost career, or a broken marriage. The separation and loss are difficult to digest. Losing a

The Battlefield of Faith

congregation family is heartbreaking, especially when false accusations are in the swirl.

7b. How did you recover from ministry-related grief?

One pastor said he relied heavily on family to carry him through the valley. Others found solace in returning to a daily prayer routine with intermittent fasting.

7c. What ways have you employed to overcome the emotions that guilt leaves in its wake?

Many read books that led them through the life changes in their ministers. Many learned to keep their emotions in check and applied more cognitive reason to their approach to their calling.

8. Have you dealt with guilt regarding your wounding?   Y or N

This question was difficult for the pastors because guilt and grief are intertwined. Again, some who had guilt did not have grief. Understanding forgiveness was the balm that began the healing process for those who dealt with guilt. If we look at sin as guilt, Scripture tells us in Romans 3:23 that all have sinned and fallen from the grace of God. So, some, but not all, pastors admitted they had a role in their woundedness. Shirking responsibility was not their aim, and the benefit of the doubt in terms of their guilt played a significant role.

8a. What instances did you face that led to your ministry-related guilt?

The most prominent thought of those who felt guilt was that they could have communicated better. Many felt that they were misled by the actions of their church governing bodies, and the expectations of the church did not match the expectations of the clergy.

8b.   How did you recover from ministry-related guilt?

Their recovery from the weight of guilt began with forgiveness, which led to redemption, which set them on a path to reset.

8c.   What ways have you employed to overcome the emotions that guilt leaves in its wake?

Again, most pastors employed mind over matter and gained much wisdom, which may be an easily missed strength and blessing.

Part VI. Anxiety/Fear.

Navigating out of guilt and grief often leads to anxiety which can manifest in fear of the unknown, the future, job security, church responsibilities, and fear of God. The doubt resurfaces, and the wounded question their calling and ministry.

9.   Do you ever feel anxious or fearful?   Y or N

The pastors were mixed on this question. Some felt fearful at times, some anxious at times, and some respondents felt both.

9a.   What steps do you take to calm your anxiety or fear?

One took steps to allay his fears and anxiety by relaxing with his spouse, singing songs of praise, reviewing the good things God did in his life, and infrequently but at times, taking a drink. Another took long walks around the neighborhood. Another engaged in exercise, while another rested and listened to calming music. Another pastor held long conversations with his trusted friends to alleviate his anxiety and stress.

9b.   Does courage enable you to confront anxiety or fear?

All the pastors relied on scripture to gain the upper hand over anxiety and fear. The most referenced scriptural passage was Deuteronomy 31:15, which says, "Be strong and courageous. Do not be afraid or terrified because of them, for the Lord your God goes with you; he will never leave or forsake you." This was followed by Joshua 1:6, "Be strong and courageous, because you will lead these people to inherit the land that I swore to their ancestors to give them."

9c.   Does this stage strengthen/weaken your relationship with God?   S or W

All pastors felt that this stage of fear and anxiety motivated them through the valley.

Part VII. Faith/Trust.

By God's grace, the clergy who have journeyed this far have reached the safety net. Lesser clergy opt out as defeated soldiers of the cross. This is the turning point where clergy gets back the joy of being in God's service.

10.   Have you felt the battles were worth the effort in your challenges?   Y or N

All pastors reported in the affirmative.

10a. Did you become stronger from your wounded experiences?   Y or N

All pastors reported in the affirmative.

10b. Would you travel this road again?   Y or N

10c. (1) If NO, why? One reported that he would not travel this road again because he believed people are unlikely to change, causing him great pain.

10d. (2) If YES, why? Another reported that he would not go through this again. Yet, if he ventured on this path again, he knew the outcome would be different. He believed developing a more vital spirit would be worth the trouble.

10e. Would you change anything?   Y or N

The one who answered no said that although he couldn't change people, he knew God could change them for the better. All other pastors reported they would keep everything the same.

10f. (1) If YES, what?

10g. Was your faith increased?   Y or N

All pastors reported that their faith was stronger from the experience.

10h. (1) If NO, how does it decrease or stagnate?

10i. (2) If YES, how? There was a consensus among the pastors that their trust in God caused them to yield to him in all that they did.

Part VIII Hope/Joy.

"But I have prayed for you that your faith may not fail. And when you have turned again, strengthen your brothers."[186] Peter must have suffered through all the stages under discussion. Still, after the abject failure, his future ministry would be as the leader of the 1st Century Church. He could never have hoped for the joy of such an impact on Christ.

11. Do you believe God uses your history to create future ministry? Y or N

    All pastors felt God used their past to prepare them for ministry.

    11a. What were the circumstances surrounding renewed hope of future ministry?

    (When, Where, How?) One said his ministry is focused on bringing opportunity to the less fortunate. He serves three churches as a bi-vocational minister.

    11b. How does your current ministry hope differ from your pre-wounded ministry?

    One said that his ministry is more intentional due to the challenges he faced early in his ministry. In some ways, he had developed a thick skin to the frequent attacks in daily ministry. He replies that staying in the word is crucial to staying connected to his ministry.

    11c. How is hope in your current ministry similar to your pre-wounded ministry?

12. What do you enjoy most about your current ministry?

---

[186] Luke 22:32.

Part VIII. Peace/ Victory

Peace is the absence of war or chaos. John 14:27, "I am leaving you with a gift—peace of mind and heart. And the peace I give is a gift the world cannot give. So do not be troubled or afraid." Isaiah 40:31 says, "But those who hope in the Lord will renew their strength. They will soar on wings like eagles; they will run and not grow weary; they will walk and not be faint." Ministry is not for the faint of heart.

Final Comments:

Q: What curricula would you recommend as help to wounded ministers?

"Daily Devotions"

Q: How can wounded ministers be recruited for their needed help?

"Sharing our story."

Q: What are your thoughts/opinions on these Seven Stages of Reset?

"It is helpful to all of us."

"I was expecting something that more closely approximated recognition and treatment of the stages of grief."

Q: Do you think the Seven Stages are helpful for the clergy? For laity? For other professions?

"For all categories."

"Professionals are most likely to benefit from this, as their profession and identities are closely tied."

Q: What recommendations would you make to improve this Seven Stage Reset?

"Spending time with God is so important that we should do it more than now."

This ends the questionnaire and responses.

Summary

This exercise is not scientific, but it successfully illustrates many challenges pastors face worldwide. Those pastors who participated should be complimented for their contribution to this experiment. A fascinating result of this exercise is that it validates the Pastoral Care, Inc. survey, which was reported in Chapter One. If nothing else is revealed, all will agree that the work to build the kingdom of God is difficult. If anyone sees the work of ministry as a life of leisure and pain-free, that person is wrongly mistaken. This is why the ministry is a call.

Anyone working in the vineyards is not for the faint of heart. It takes guts and determination. Stuart Briscoe is quoted as saying, "Qualifications of a pastor: the mind of a scholar, the heart of a child, and the hide of a rhinoceros."[187] Many pastors fall and are wounded. If it comes to fruition, Slains Ministries' desires that many fallen wounded soldiers for Christ will be reset and returned to the field to fight another day.

---

[187] Stuart Briscoe Quotes. https://quotefancy.com/quote/1581972/Stuart-Briscoe-Qualifications-of-a-pastor-the-mind-of-a-scholar-the-heart-of-a-child-and-the-hide-of-a-rhinoceros.

CHAPTER SIX

The Literature Review

Kirk Byron Jones, *Rest in The Storm* (King of Prussia: Judson Press Publishers, 2021).

This 20th-anniversary edition offers many tools for combating the storms of ministry, including emotional, physical, and spiritual. From these tools, one can find more balance in ministry and life. The source focuses on rest and renewal and draws from biblical narratives. Jones offers practical wisdom from thirty years of pastoral ministry. He highlights the gifts of stillness, friendship, creativity, and laughter for enriching ones are chosen vocations.

Coupled with these insights, he advises building meaningful relationships between ministry leaders and caregivers. Although caregivers are not the focus of Slains Ministries, it is essential to review their unique gifts, considering the wide range of duties called upon by a member of pastor's congregations.

G. Lloyd Rediger, *Clergy Killers: Guidance for Pastors and Congregations Under Attack* (Louisville: Westminster John Knox Press, 1997).

This author complements K.B. Jones's book because it identifies the regular storms of a minister's life and guides pastors under attack. Rediger provides a reasoned approach to ministry by revealing what many church members would rather not mention that churches are often in conflict. In Goodreads, Abigail Van Buren said, "churches are not museums for saints, rather hospitals for sinners." This quote is used here because it underscores succinctly how much we are at odds with undercurrents that ultimately affect the minister.

By recognizing the conflicts in church life, one can address the issue to reach a reasonable conclusion where healing can commence. This source provides many insights into where clergy can begin to recover, restore, refresh, and reset. One of the interesting statistics mentioned in this source was the mental health of ministers. Burnout (exhaustion to the point of malfunction) was at the top of the list, with 15 percent for clergy and 8-12 percent for the general population.

Dennis R. Maynard, *When Sheep Attack!* (Charleston: BookSurge Publishers, 2010).

    Dennis Maynard addresses the ultimate betrayal when a church congregation turns against its shepherd. This is one of the unsavory realities of church life today. From these experiences, many willing and needy clergy are expected to find solace in the teaching, counseling, and training offered at Slains Ministries. This source cites Gene Wood, author of *Turn Around Churches,* noting that 1300 Christian pastors are forced to resign from their parishes every month, often without cause.

This action is compounded by the veil of secrecy that clouds the situation with rumors and insinuations that will haunt ministers for the remainder of their ministry. Wood says that another 1200 clergy every month leave the ministry stating stress-related issues, family anxieties, and burnout. Another source cited is Kenneth C. Haugk, who says in his book *Antagonists in the Church,* that some church members, in their quest for power, take zeal in tearing down churches. This may border on a psychological disorder.

Nevertheless, the church is open to everyone in our society who is hurting or needs healing. Thus, the shepherd becomes the "faith" healer. This is a reason to develop a place called Slains Ministries, where ministers can attend to become restored for the battles for the hearts and minds of God's people, many of whom are lost and lonely.

Paul David Tripp, *Dangerous Calling* (Wheaton: Good News Publishers, 2012).

This book puts into words the disconnected feelings among clergy and helps them understand the world they serve. It is the balm for the clergy to focus on the challenges of the ordained and vocational ministry. By identifying the enemy, ministers are better equipped to engage the evil that seems to be around every corner.

This book centers on counseling, an essential ingredient for the wounded warrior attending the retreat. Tripp also advises clergy to avoid self-righteous demonstrations and vain glory. Pastors are well advised to leave pride behind, or a sudden fall from grace could be in store for the arrogant preacher.

Fred Lehr. *Clergy Burnout: Surviving in Turbulent Times* (Minneapolis: Fortress Press, 2022).

Fred Lehr is the founder and manager of Renewal Ministries, which helps broken church professionals through instruction on conflict management, change management, establishing healthy boundaries, stress management, and growing healthy congregations. This source instructs clergy on how to (re)gain balance through nurture in continuing education, spiritual direction, clergy support groups, therapy, leisure time, (developing) friendships, and renewed confidence in one's calling.

These are essential steps in developing this project because it outlines sequential steps that build upon each other, strengthening the wounded warrior one segment at a time. The resource begins by describing and identifying the multilayered events that lead to burnout and directs the pastor toward hope and healing. These steps provide a solid healing, restoration, and reset the ministry foundation.

Rae-Jean Proeschold-Bell and Jason Byassee, *Faithful, and Fractured: Responding to the Clergy Health Crisis* (Ada: Baker Academic Publishers, 2018).

This resource is unique because its findings are carefully written and well-researched. Its mission is to understand the problems of clergy from a scientific viewpoint, while its underpinning is purely theological. It is designed for clergy health and sustainability. This book will help the future staff of Slains Ministries to connect the dots to a more rewarding experience in the proposed healing retreat.

Since pastors are creatures doing the Creator's work, it is essential to learn how to navigate the pits and perils of the vocational ministry. Performing holy duties and being accountable to God is unlike any other career. It requires a unique approach to the experience of restoration, renewal, and resetting of future clergy participants at the Slains Ministries retreat.

Roy M. Oswald, *Clergy Self-Care: Finding A Balance for Effective Ministry* (Washington: The Alban Institute Publishing, 1998).

This source leads the wounded pastor toward wholeness and provides lessons and studies that will prove invaluable as treatment plans and classes are developed at Slains Ministries. As Lutheran pastor Oswald points out, wholeness happens on four levels simultaneously, beginning with the pastor's physical and emotional (health), leading to the focus on spiritual health, and finally to our intellectual (psychological) health. All four begin with reconciling the wounded spiritual warrior to his Creator. After the repair is made, the process of healing and wholeness starts to manifest.

Pastoral group therapies are one way, but increasingly, there is a need for a structured retreat that can provide help through professional counseling and spiritual therapies that restore the wounded spiritual leader. Learning to deal with stress and anxieties, as well as learning the warning signs, is imperative to the health of a minister. Learning to say "no" is also a self-help tool. Although the Scripture tells us that "the harvest is plentiful, and the workers are few." This does not license ministers to work beyond their capacities to the point of ineffectiveness. This source is a great book to help define the roles of staff and professionals at the Slains Minister's retreat.

Matt Bloom, *Flourishing in Ministry: How to Cultivate Clergy Wellbeing* (Washington: Rowan & Littlefield Publishers, 2019).

This book is helpful because it focuses on ministers' daily well-being and teaches them resilience. There is no question that pastors need to be resilient in their approach to ministry because it is a high-stakes vocation, and it is often complex and diverse. There is no typical day in the life of a pastor. Learning to cope with the demands of Sunday worship coupled with hospital visitations and unexpected events which make one pivot, pastoral counseling, weddings, and funerals can be an overwhelming way of life.

Finding one's well-being and remaining healthy in body, mind, and spirit is paramount in the life of a Christian minister. Developing traits that sustain and provide daily well-being may provide years of joyful and rewarding experiences. Prioritizing one's workload and pace is vital for well-being during cultural and ecclesiastical challenges and changes.

Bloom provides insights into the work of pastors, which is often stressful, underappreciated, unforgiving, and financially challenging. The work of the ministry is so demanding that sometimes the needs of the ministers are sacrificed for the needs of congregations. Bloom provides practical insights for clergies who navigate the complex challenges of ministry.

Making time for rest is crucial for the health and well-being of ministers who too often risk their health to care for their church members. Bloom's advice helps ministers to flourish in their ministries if they follow his ways forward chart. Many of the tenets found in this source will be helpful in the development of foundational resources needed to provide a positive experience at Slains Ministries.

Eugene H. Peterson, *The Contemplative Pastor: Returning to the Art of Spiritual Direction* (Grand Rapids: Eerdmans Publishing, 1993).

E. H. Peterson helps redefine the meaning of being a pastor in three categories, which are unbusy, subversive, and apocalyptic. From examining man's will and God's will to finding oneself in the desert and entering a sabbatical, Peterson draws on years of experience and wisdom on the challenges of ministers. This source provides an out-of-the-box observation of ministry, which is revealing and refreshing. Its tenets leave the reader to refit for the vocation of ministry. This is a vital source for training the trainers at the Slains Ministry.

Michael and Kathy Langston, *A Journey of Hope* (Silverton: Lampion Press, LLC, 2016).

Authors Michael and Kathy Langston provide a personal account of a journey of hope. USN retired Captain Michael Langston outlines his military career and the lessons learned. From the battlefields of Iraq and Afghanistan, he came home with combat stress and fatigue. His first-hand trauma later developed into PTSD. After enduring a season of intensive counseling, he was able to mitigate his challenges and redirect the positive energy to good use.

As a college professor, he has learned to face the challenges of post-traumatic stress and teach his students ways and therapies how to cope with its symptoms and corral them so they can lead a productive life. Much of the ministry of Slains will be working with pastors who, from the spiritual battlefield, face their definition of PTSD.

Kathy Langston's contribution to this book is distinctly helpful because, as a wounded warrior's spouse, she knows the marriage partner's unique challenges. Her insight can help pastors' wives in their journey to hope. *A Journey of Hope* leads the wounded warrior into a place of respite where they can refresh, restore, and reset their lives and be productive again.

Elie Wiesel, *Night* (New York: Hill and Wang, 1958).

This book was included in this study because it represents many aspects that clergy face when navigating through the seven reset stages. When a pastor falls off his perch willingly or unwillingly, he reaches a bottom where all hope, purpose, and value are gone. This is a lonely place where all seems lost. Elie Wiesel knows what this place looks and feels like. He experienced it from the horrific events of the Holocaust. He demonstrated in this book that one can survive despite the trauma of loss, betrayal, failure, family, and soul. *Night* is a book about survival.

Pastors who experience dejection, cancellation, and abandonment from their creator, they think, can recover and reset to become productive members of the ministry and society again. *Night* is a remarkable book that can inspire the worst cases of clergy burnout.

Clive Staples Lewis, *The Weight of Glory* (New York: Harper-Collins, 1949).

Perhaps the most significant Christian apologist of the twentieth century is former atheist C.S. Lewis. *The Weight of Glory* is taken from his notes from his Cambridge class lectures that made their way into book form. The title says it all. For members of the clergy, the weight of ministry can be overwhelming. The author speaks uniquely about what is on people's minds but cannot verbalize it in conversation.

Lewis found a way to translate people's thoughts and converse with them. His insightful ability to see into the hearts and minds of his students is remarkable. He is part theologian, part psychologist. His take on the inner rings is straight from life's underbelly, which means he can interpret street knowledge and transform it into cognitive theories. By this, he can interpret the wolf in all of humanity.

This knowledge is pertinent to the best uses of all clergy, for many would not have become wounded if they had a better grasp of each person's carnal desires and devices. His commentary is that we expect better from Christian people, but far too often, clergy must learn lessons the hard way.

Viktor E. Frankl, *Man's Search for Meaning* (Boston: Beacon Press, 1959).

Like Elie Wiesel, Viktor Frankl was a product of the Holocaust. There are valuable lessons from the debts of despair and loss of hope. Like Wiesel, Frankl survived the death camps and lost most of his family. When tragedy and trauma drop a person to these unimaginable depths, the ability to find a morsel of wisdom or a glimmer of light compels the reader to connect to that person.

This book benefits from the experience of Viktor Frankl. As a medical doctor and psychologist, he could look into the soul of humanity, where few have ventured. This perspective or introspective ability has significant use for wounded clergy who feel all is lost.

Frankl's thesis that humanity's motivation is a search for purpose answers humanity's question: why? It surpasses Sigmund Freud's theory of pleasure and Arthur Adler's theory of power and connects to humanity in a way no other person has. This book is a valuable resource for clergy who venture to the Slains Clergy Retreat.

Phyllis Tickle, *The Great Emergence: How Christianity is Changing and Why* (Grand Rapids: Baker Books, 2012).

Phyllis Tickle has found a compelling explanation of the church today and surmises where it might go. She begins her treatise from history lessons, which provides a foundation for her theories and strengthens her arguments. It is as good an explanation as anyone currently analyzing the disintegrating or converging church as we know it from alternating viewpoints.

One of her status bars is the quadrilateral of Liturgical, Social Justice Christians, Renewalists, and Conservatives. She uses this prism to examine the various segments of the church as it evolves. The church essentially is a big umbrella of doctrines and worship expressions. The book is helpful for clergy by giving a perspective of the church and providing a roadmap to navigate future ministries.

Dietrich Bonhoeffer, *The Cost of Discipleship* (New York: Touchstone, 1995).

This is one of the twentieth century's five most influential Christian books. Dietrich Bonhoeffer's book is an inspired effort to illuminate the cost of ministry for clergy and disciples of all stripes. His argument forms around the contrasting elements of cheap grace and costly grace. While he gave the ultimate price for costly grace, he compels his readers and students to examine their faith in a way not many theologians can muster.

The cost of discipleship can be more than many can pay, but it is worth the expense for those who do. This book will be an ongoing requirement for those who attend Slains Clergy Retreat. It helps wounded clergy reexamine first their salvation and then their calling. It is a must for any serious member of the clergy.

Rae-Jean Proeschold-Bell and Jason Byassee, *Faithful, and Fractured: Responding to the Clergy Health Crisis* (Grand Rapids: Baker Academic, 2018).

Proeschold-Bell and Byassee look at the highs and lows of ministry in the context of being faithful and fractured. Their work looks at the results of clergy burnout and how it often leads to depression. The authors provide treatment solutions to improve pastors' emotional and spiritual health and well-being. This is a companion book for navigating the seven stages of reset described in this book.

This is as much a clinical product as a narrative for the health of ministers in crisis. One of the main proposals is a practical guide for combating stress and its associated symptoms. Another point is the need for a positive attitude, especially regarding emotions. Keeping one's emotions in check will help the pastor gain cognitive strength to combat the challenges facing a modern-day minister. This is a valuable source for Slains Ministries.

Joni Eareckson Tada and Steven Estes, *When God Weeps: Why Our Sufferings Matter to the Almighty* (Grand Rapids: Zondervan, 1977).

Joni Tada and Steven Estes answer one of humanity's most important questions. From Jesus to Wiesel to Frankl to Tada, we have all wrestled with the thought of a loving and just God allowing bad things to happen to good people. Joni was paralyzed from a diving accident as a teenager and became a quadriplegic.

She has authored several books about her trials and struggles as a personal example of God's grace. Joni challenges the reader to open a dialogue with God by asking who he is, what he is up to, and where he is going. The answers to these questions unravel the reason for a pastor's burnout and begin the road to recovery. There is no better example of grace than Joni Tada, whose life story can give hope to wounded pastors.

Marcus J. Borg, *The Heart of Christianity: Rediscovering a Life of Faith* (New York: Harper One, 1989).

Marcus J. Borg says that the heart of Christianity is changing, and it is not as simple as being liberal or conservative. The Christian church and our faith are enduring a time of change and conflict. His contribution to this study highlights the changes prominent in the marketplace of theology and the world.

He addressed three examples that are at the heart of the debate in the church today. These issues are 1) Ordination of women, 2) Gays and Lesbians, and 3) Christian exclusivism. On the ordination of women, he notes that over half of those attending seminary today are women. About gays and lesbians, he says that the debate is not centered on gays and lesbians being married but on whether they can be ordained as clergy.

For Christian exclusivism, Borg writes that the conventional wisdom is that there are more ways to salvation than through one exclusive religion because the statistics say it is so. I included this study because it covers the hot issues facing clergy today. Many reasons there is a significant exit from the ministry are these three contentious issues facing the church. Knowing our enemy is a strength that needs to be understood, and this book helps to understand the challenges pastors face regarding these issues.

H. Norman Wright, *Helping Those in Grief* (Ventura: Regal Books, 2010).

    H. Norman Wright is a licensed marriage and family therapist. He is a Research Professor of Christian Education at the Talbot School of Theology. He is the author of seventy books and has been involved in this vocation for over forty years of clinical and classroom experience. This book is included because Wright is a grief expert. Grief is one of the conditions that wounded clergy will experience when they face leaving the ministry God called them to do.
    Wright says that ministers are called to the pastoral vocation, where they will care for people who are facing hardship, trauma, and loss. His book provides many case studies and helps the student learn techniques that guide them in asking the right questions and giving the correct answers. This book is unique because it helps the parishioner and the pastor.

Robert D. Dale, *To Dream Again, Again!* (Macon: Nurturing Faith Incorporated, 2018).

    Robert Dale says that ministry is a moving target. He is right because the ministry is constantly changing. He points out that churches should provide a contrast to the culture rather than be in comparison to the culture. The author has focused his writings on church leadership and church ministries.
    His main objective is to keep churches invigorated and moving upward. He provides a bell curve that follows a church plant that begins with a dream, beliefs, goals, structure, and then a fully mature ministry. If that congregation becomes stagnant, it becomes nostalgic,

questioning, polarizing, dropout, and closure. This bell curve is a warning sign for congregations and pastors to remain vigilant and not let their congregation fall into the valley of no return.

Tim Clinton and Joshua Straub, *God Attachment* (New York: Howard Books, 2010).

Authors Clinton and Straub ask the difficult questions at the heart of wounded pastors that begin with, why? Then the wounded ask if there is a God and does he matter. Their book starts from the premise of a crisis of belief. Then they assemble the puzzle, identifying that humanity's makeup centers on hardware and software. Their premise continues this narrative that humanity was made for relationships. They analyze why relationships go wrong not only individually but corporately in the family of God, the church.

This book is helpful because it explains who pastors are and how they connect to their world and congregations. When things get out of order, the pursuit of intimacy through reset and renewal with God is a source of healing. This book offers many insights for wounded clergy in their restoration.

Timothy Keller, *Center Church* (Grand Rapids: Zondervan, 2012).

Prolific religious writer and study group developer Timothy Keller incorporates all his life experiences in producing Center Church. It is his version of the church of tomorrow. He is commended for putting forth a view of the church that personally transforms a community by relating to followers. He does not cower from the complex tenets of Scripture and lays the groundwork for many issues a future cleric may face in their ministry.

This book is included because it provides a prophetic view of what church is and will be in the future. Wounded clergy need a bird's eye view of the landscape regarding the future challenges they will undoubtedly face. This book is perhaps the most significant of Keller's offerings regarding the pragmatic church.

Henri J. M. Nouwen, *Wounded Healer: Ministry in Contemporary Society* (New York: Random House, 1972).

Roman Catholic priest Henri Nouwen, a Notre Dame, Yale, and Harvard professor, pens a simple book in many ways before its time. He pushes the boundaries of church hierarchy and argues that church is about relationships where clergy connect to their parishioners from the standpoint of their pain. There are threads of Christ woven in this narrative because ministers are wounded, helping the wounded.

Many pastors begin their ministries from a position of weakness rather than strength. There is strength in this paradox because, as Paul says, we are weak, but he (Jesus) is strong. Even Jesus has projected a sense of weakness or, shall we say, meekness that is often viewed as weak and ineffective.

On the contrary, it is precisely the formula that connects the wounded in this world that netted together provides a vitality and spiritual fullness that is not acquired any other way. This book is thought-provoking in many ways and is an excellent resource for wounded warriors.

Clive Staples Lewis, *The Problem of Pain* (New York: HarperCollins Publishers, 1996).

C.S. Lewis, one of the most essential Christian apologists of the twentieth century, writes about the problem of pain, not the problem with pain. This perspective is essential because it gets to the root of pain, not treating it as only a symptom. Like many of his contributions, this book was compiled from class lectures.

Lewis discusses the nature of death while addressing the Christian tenets of trials and tribulations followed by pain and suffering. He also examines man's relationship with God and how it becomes strained when pain enters the equation. His view of Christ's crucifixion helps everyone consider the challenges we face when doing all that is necessary to justify the death of God's only son and make sense of it.

All this is done so that his creation of man follows in the steps of God's purpose for humanity. Wars and rumors of wars that lead to destruction, including the death of animals, are considered. His treatise on hell is akin to Dante's *Inferno*, where man will find himself without a relationship with God. Of all the problems of pain, it is theoretically found in the grips of Hades, which humanity should take steps to avoid. This narrative is helpful for Slains ministries because it examines pain and places it in proper perspective yielding to a reset with God.

Stephen T. Davis, *Encountering Evil: Live Options in Theodicy* (Louisville: Westminster John Knox Press, 2001).

Stephen Davis edits this group of essays from theologians and religious commentators who write about the problems with evil. This compilation is offered from a wide range of thoughts and viewpoints. It represents the vindication of God from a broad spectrum of views and contrasts and compares their impact on the religious community. From Creation to Free Will to Irenaean philosophy, this narrative presents the complex problems evil creates.

This book is helpful in the wounded warrior because it exposes alternate views that open the minds of those who need to know how and why pastors fight the good fight.

Gary L. McIntosh and Samuel D. Rima, *Overcoming the Dark Side of Leadership: How to Become an Effective Leader by Confronting Potential Failures: Revised Edition* (Grand Rapids: Baker Books, 2007).

These authors provide insight into the challenges of leadership. A pastor is more than a spiritual discerner; he is a leader. The business side of the church is just as important as the theological messages preachers brought weekly to their congregations.

Additionally, McIntosh and Rima suggest that there is a dark side to every person. Knowing a pastor's strengths and weaknesses can either elevate a ministry or hinder a pastor's ministry. Another view of this dark side is a level of narcissism. The enemy is strong and has many battle elements, such as tanks, aircraft, and infantry, in the form of gossip, temptation, and a sense of worthlessness. Much of this is ingrained in a pastor's childhood. How these tendencies manifest into adulthood is paramount to the success of a pastor's ministry. The author asks if it is possible to rid oneself of this dark side, but not in the same vein as one who considers that our shadows go away at night only to return in daylight.

This is a good example that we can only reach an incomplete level of righteousness. Yet, it should not prevent the productive ministry possible in all pastors if they learn to keep their dark side in check. This book helps wounded pastors understand the boundaries of ministry.

David Kinnaman and Mark Matlock, *Faith for Exiles: Five Ways for a New Generation to Follow Jesus in Digital Babylon* (New York: Baker Books, 2019).

Kinnaman and Matlock provide an informing narrative of the world as it is transitioning into the digital age, which they term Digital Babylon. Every generation has experienced innovation and new products that change our lives. An example of this change is no better described as people leaving the horse and buggy and embracing the automobile around the turn of the last century.

Another example was adopting electricity instead of whale oil to keep the lanterns burning or lit. The church today is in the midst of another cataclysmic event with the advent of modes of communication in the one-dimensional arena. No longer does the latest generation yearn for a three-dimensional activity. Church leaders must find a way to communicate with smartphones, tablets, laptops, and computers, including sound systems.

This digital world is not limited to electronic devices; it is incumbent on pastors to learn to communicate through social media, from Facebook to Twitter to Google. Learning the changing landscape is part of the treatment plans for Slains Ministries.

Alister McGrath, *Heresy: A History of Defending the Truth* (London: Society for Promoting Christian Knowledge, 2009).

Rick Warren, the author of *The Purpose Driven Life*, writes that the insights provided in *Heresy* are compelling and comprehensive. Indeed, they are insightful and enlightening. Many say that knowledge is growing exponentially. If so, the driving force to a world of knowledge is accessed by our personal computers and handheld computers, the smartphone. Until the latest generation, knowledge was found on dusty shelves hidden in great libraries worldwide.

Now that this information is being digitized, it is being received by many hands. Many of the heresies of the ancient past are now being viewed and reviewed again and gaining popularity. The value of McGrath's book is to shed light on the heresies of the past and refresh the new audiences of their danger, especially regarding church theology and doctrine.

This book is another example of the battlefields facing pastors. A general knowledge and appreciation of these heresies is helpful to know the enemy and be prepared to confront and defeat them.

Avery Cardinal Dulles, *Models of the Church* (New York: Random House, 2002).

The author provides six models of the church, which include Mystical Communion (Emphasis on the Spirit), Sacrament (Word and Sacrament), Servant (Commitment to social justice), Herald (Proclaiming the Gospel and Evangelizing), Institution (Hierarchal), and Community of Disciples (Followers of Jesus). These six models cover the broad range of Christian practices inherent in congregations.

The latest model is the Community of Disciples. This model incorporates the current buzzword among potential adherents to organized worship. It encourages its followers to be more like Jesus in their daily walk. This model has ushered in a movement for independent non-denominational churches to begin planting.

However, this model lacks a connection to the universal church. This contribution to this book is meaningful because it identifies the main models of the church. Knowing these different groups helps develop avenues for treatment for wounded warriors.

John Bunyan, *The Pilgrim's Progress: From This World and That Which Is to Come* (New York: Barnes & Noble Classics, 2005).

Arguably, this is one of the classic books of English literature. This book is all the more fascinating, given that the author wrote this while in prison on less-than-stellar charges. John Bunyan is a master of the human mind and spirit. This story focuses on the temptations and trials of the main character, Christian, who journeys from this world to the next.

Bunyan's work is timeless and relates to all people of faith. He addresses Pride, Envy, Faith, Hope, and Mercy and provides an escape from their grip. His remarkable ability to see the challenges inherent in our world and draw on the spiritual gifts that transform us from flesh to spiritual beings is worth analysis.

This creative story is helpful to the wounded clergy because it addresses the internal issues faced with a common touch that ushers the minister into a place of acceptance without condemnation. This is a valuable source for healing wounded pastors.

APPENDIX

Seven Stage Reset

Questionnaire

Part I: Preset - Starting Point.

13. Do you believe the Christian church and ministry are in crisis?   Y or N

14. Have you ever considered leaving your ministry for another vocation?   Y or N

   2a. If so, what were the circumstances?

   2b. What did you do to mitigate the circumstances?

   2c. How did you overcome the challenges you faced?

15. Could a ministry of healing help wounded ministers stay in service?   Y or N

   3a. What had the most profound effect on healing wounds you received in ministry?

Part II. Pride/Vanity.

Proverbs 13:10 states that pride leads to a fall. The world advocates a quest for power, prestige, fame, and fortune.

16. Did pride play any part in your ministry wounding or decline? Y or N

    4a. If so, what happened?

    4b. How were you reset?

    4c. Did you receive help (professional or non-professional) to reset?

    4d. Or did you make the journey to reset on your own?

Part III. Doubt/Depression.

Left unabated, doubts can lead to depression. A protracted state of depression, if it becomes clinical, can lead to debilitation.

17. Did doubt visit you in your journey as a wounded clergy? Y or N

    5a. Were (or are) any lasting effects of doubt on your upward recovery?

    5b. What is the status of your journey toward healing (professional or personal)?

    5c. How did you navigate to a better place?

    5d. List the steps you took, in chronological order, if you can.

Part IV. Temptation/Addiction.

The Bible declares that we all face temptation, sometimes leading to addictions. Addiction knows no boundaries and can be almost anything. Consider addiction as 'idol worship' to help form your answers.

18. In your wounded state, did you develop any addictions? Y or N

    6a. If yes, what can you tell us about it?

    6b. How did it affect your church, family, and ministry?

    6c. How did you recover from your addiction(s)?

    6d. Do you still struggle with addiction(s)?

Part V. Guilt/Despair.

Often, we review our history with heavy hearts and deep regrets. This is the essence of guilt and grief. Guilt or grief can lead to spiritual paralysis and ultimately affects ministries.

19. Have you dealt with grief regarding your wounding? Y or N

    7a. What instances did you face that led to your ministry-related grief?

    7b. How did you recover from ministry-related grief?

    7c. What ways have you employed to overcome the emotions that guilt leaves in its wake?

20. Have you dealt with guilt regarding your wounding?   Y or N

    8a. What instances did you face that led to your ministry-related guilt?

    8b. How did you recover from ministry-related guilt?

    8c. What ways have you employed to overcome the emotions that guilt leaves in its wake?

Part VI. Anxious/Fear.

Navigating out of guilt and grief often leads to anxiety which can manifest in fear of the unknown, the future, job security, church responsibilities, and fear of God. The doubt resurfaces, and the wounded question their calling and ministry.

21. Do you ever feel anxious or fearful?   Y or N

    9a. What steps do you take to calm your anxiety or fear?

    9b. Does courage enable you to confront anxiety or fear?

    9c. Does this stage strengthen/weaken your relationship with God?   S or W

Part VII. Faith/Trust.

By God's grace, the clergy who have journeyed this far have reached the safety net. Lesser clergy opt out as defeated soldiers of the cross. This is the turning point where clergy gets back the joy of being in God's service.

22. Have you felt the battles were worth the effort in your challenges?   Y or N

    10a. Did you become more substantial from your wounded experiences?   Y or N

    10b. Would you travel this road again?   Y or N

        10b. (1) If NO, why?

        10b. (2) If YES, why?

    10c. Would you change anything?   Y or N

        10c. (1) If YES, what?

    10d. Was your faith increased?   Y or N

        10d. (1) If NO, how does it decrease or stagnate?

        10d. (2) If YES, how?

Part VIII. Hope/Joy.

"But I have prayed for you that your faith may not fail. And when you have turned again, strengthen your brothers." Peter must have suffered through all the stages under discussion. Still, after the abject failure, his future ministry would be as the leader of the 1st Century Church. He could never have hoped for the joy of such an impact on Christ.

23. Do you believe God uses your history to create future ministry?   Y or N

11a. What were the circumstances surrounding renewed hope of future ministry?

(When, Where, How?)

11b. How does your current ministry hope differ from your pre-wounded ministry?

11c. How is your current ministry hope similar to your pre-wounded ministry?

24. What do you enjoy most about your current ministry?

Part VIII. Hope/Peace/Joy. Victory and Ministry.

Peace is the absence of war or chaos. John 14:27, "I am leaving you with a gift—peace of mind and heart. And the peace I give is a gift the world cannot give. So do not be troubled or afraid." Isaiah 40:31, "But those who hope in the Lord will renew their strength. They will soar on wings like eagles; they will run and not grow weary; they will walk and not be faint." Ministry is not for the faint of heart.

FINAL COMMENTS:

Q: What curricula would you recommend as help to wounded ministers?

Q: How can wounded ministers be recruited for their needed help?

Q: What are your thoughts/opinions on these Seven Stages of Reset?

Q: Do you think Seven Stages are helpful for the clergy? For laity? For other professions?

Q: What recommendations would you make to improve this Seven Stage Reset?

BIBLIOGRAPHY

Anglican American Council. "Clergy Care and Wellness," Accessed September 7, 2021, https://americananglican.org/project/for-clergy/.

Andreasen, Nancy C. *"What is Post-traumatic Stress Disorder?"* Published online: April 01, 2022. Pages 240-243. https://www.tanddonline.com/doi/full/10.3187/DCNS.2011.13.2/nandresen.

Ashley, J. Phillip. Daniel Leadership Institute. Accessed April 3, 2023. https://americananglican.org?daniel-leadership-institute/.

Bailenson Jeremy N. *"Nonverbal Overload: A Theoretical Argument for The Causes of Zoom Fatigue."* Accessed November 12, 2022. https://psycnet.apa > record.

Barna Group. "A New Chapter in Millennial Church Attendance." Articles in Faith & Christianity, https://barna.com/research, Accessed December 10, 2022.

Barna, George. *The Second Coming of The Church*. Nashville: Thomas Nelson, Inc., 1998.

Barth, Karl. *Homiletics*. Westminster John Knox Press, 1991.

Bolt, Robert. *"Franklin Delano Roosevelt, Senior Warden, St. James Church at Hyde Park, New York."* Historical Magazine of the

Protestant Episcopal Church, 54 no. 1 (1985). http://www.jstor.org/stable/42974061.

Bonhoeffer, Dietrich. *The Cost of Discipleship* New York: Simon & Schuster, 1995.

BookBrowse.com/expressions/detail/index.cfm/expression_number/238/you-can-run-but-you-can't-hide. Accessed February 12, 2023. https://www.bookbrowse.com >detail

Borg, Marcus J. *The Heart of Christianity Rediscovering a Life of Faith*. New York: Harper One, 2003.

Brown, Jon. *"Nearly One-third Of Churches Split from Regional Methodist Church Body Amid Ongoing Schism About Sexuality."* Fox News. Accessed January 10, 2022. https://www.foxnews.com/us/nearly-one-third-churches-split-regional-methodist-church-body-amid-ongoing-schism-about-sexuality.

Bullock, Richard, and Richard Bruesehoff. *Clergy Renewal: The Alban Guide to Sabbatical Planning*. Rowan & Littlefield, 2000.

Bunyan, John. *The Pilgrim's Progress* New York: Barnes & Nobel Classics, 2005.

Burrows, Millar. *Jesus in The First Three Gospels*. Nashville: Abingdon, 1977.

Cambridge English Dictionary. "*A Wolf in Sheep's Clothing,*" Accessed January 24, 2022. https://dictionary.cambridge.org/us/dictionary/english-chinese-traditional/a-wolf-in-sheep-s-clothing.

Cleveland Clinic. *Burnout: % Signs and What to Do about It*. Accessed October 11, 2022. health.clevelandclinic.org.

Call2Disciple. John Miller. Accessed April 29, 2023. https://www.call2disciple.com/john-miller.

_____. Teresa Glenn. Accessed April 29, 2023. https://www.call2disciple.com/teresa-glenn.

Cedars Sinai "Clinical Pastoral Education Program," Accessed October 5, 2021, https://www.cedars-sinai.org/patients-visitors/spiritual-care/clinicalpastoral-education.html.

Church of Wales, "Introduction to the Cure of Souls (1996): The Church and its Ministry," Accessed October 5, 2021. www.churchinwales.org.uk/en/clergy-and-members/clergy-handbook/introduction_cure_or_souls_1996/.

Christian Martyrs NOW. Accessed May 20, 2023. https://earlychurchhistory.org/martyrs/christian-martyrs-now/.

Chibi, Andrew Allan. *The Wheat and the Tares: Doctrines of the Church in the Reformation, 1500-1590*. Eugene: Wipf and Stock Publishers, 2015.

Clinton, Tim, and Joshua Straub. *God Attachment-When You Believe, Act, And Feel the Way You Do God*, New York: Simon & Shuster, Inc., 2010.

Culbertson, Rod. *The Disciple Investing Apostle: Paul's Ministry of Relationships*. Vol. 3 Eugene: Wipf and Stock Publishers, 2018.

Dale, Robert D. *To Dream Again, Again,* Macon: Nurturing Faith Publishing, 2018.

Daniel J. Treier and Uche Anizor. *Theological Interpretation of Scripture and Evangelical Systematic Theology: Iron Sharpening Iron.* Southern Baptist Journal of Theology, 2010: 4-17.

Davis, Stephen T., Editor. *Encountering Evil Live Options in Theodicy a New Edition, Louisville:* Westminster John Knox Press, 2001.

DeRoco, Chris, *By His Stripes We Are Healed: Meaning and Importance of Isaiah 53:5.*

Dictionary.com *"Storm Trooper Definition & Meaning,"* Accessed March 30, 2023. https://www.dictionary.com>browse.

Duffy, Lorraine, Alex Bordetsky, Eric Bach, Ryan Blazevich, and Carl Oros. *A Model of Tactical Battle Rhythm.* San Diego: Space and Naval Warfare Systems Command, 2004. PowerPoint Presentation.

Dulles, Cardinal Avery. *Models of the Church.* New York, Random House, 2002.

Edgecomb, Jarred. "Spurgeon on Worldliness in the Church."Faithlife Sermons. Accessed September 11, 2022. https://sermons.faithlife.com/sermons/89943-spurgeon-on-worldliness-in-the-church.

Episcopal Diocese of North Carolina, "Sabbaticals," Accessed September 31, 2021, https://www.episdionc.org/sabbaticals/.

Eskridge, Larry. *God's Forever Family: The Jesus People Movement in America.* New York: Oxford University Press USA, 2013.

Espinosa, Miguel, Akhil llango, and Giorgio Zanarone. *Sleeping with the Enemy: How Politicians and Interest Groups Adapt their Collaborations in the Face of Reputational Threats.* Preprint submitted 2022, https://www.researchgate.net/publication/361017862.

Frankl, Viktor E. *Man's Search for Meaning,* Boston: Beacon Press, 1959.

Frei, Hans W. *The Identity of Jesus Christ. Expanded and Updated Edition. The Hermeneutical Bases of Dogmatic Theology.* Eugene: Wipf and Stock Publishers, 2013.

Gillett, Charlie. *The Sound of the City: The Rise of Rock & Roll.* Accessed November 9, 2022. https://books.google.vg/books?id=Mx-nAgAAQBAJ&sitesec+reviews.

GotQuestions.org. "How Can Believers Be in The World but Not of This World?" Accessed September 02, 2022. https://www.gotquestions.org/in-but-not-of-world

_____. "What does it mean that pride goes before a fall - Proverbs 16:18?" Accessed November 15, 2022. https://www.gotquestions.org/pride-goes-before-a-fall.html.

_____. "What does it mean to become all things to all people - I Corinthians 9:22?" Accessed December 30, 2022. https://www.gotquestions.org/all-things-to-all-people.hmtl.

Graham, Billy, "Billy Graham Training Center at the Cove," Billy Graham Evangelistic Association," Accessed November 5, 2021. https://www.billygraham.org.

Handel, George Frideric, Alfred Mann, and Charles Jennens. *Messiah.* Rutgers University Documents of Music and Continuo Music Press, Inc., 1989.

Hanegraaff, Wouter J. *New Age Religion and Western Culture: Esotericism in The Mirror of Secular Thought.* New York: Suny Press. 1997.

Harding, Jr., Edward P. "Keeping the connection: An examination of the perils and benefits of a church connected 501c3 (non-profit) corporation." Ph.D. diss., Hartford Seminary, 1993. ProQuest dissertations (9532791).

Hershey, Doug. *Yeshua: The Meaning of the Hebrew Name of Jesus – FIRM Israel,* Accessed December 10, 2022. https://firmisrael.org/learn/who-is-yeshua-meaning-of-hebrew-name-jesus/.

Hilgemann, Brandon. ProPreacher.com. April 12, 2018, Assessed May 10, 2023. https://www.propreacher.com/the-one-mistake-all-preachers-make/.

Hillerbrand, Hans J. *The Protestant Reformation: Rev. Edition.* United Kingdom: HarperCollins, 2009.

Hubbard, Maggie. The D.L. Moody Center. Anxiety, depression, and the Christian life. Accessed May 12, 2023, https://moodycenter.org > articles.

Inc.com. "17 Inspiring Quotes to Help You Face Your Fears," Accessed March 14, 2023, https://www.inc.com > Sims-Wyeth.

Jones, Kirk Byron. *Rest in The Storm: Self-Care Strategies for Clergy and Other Caregivers—King* of Prussia: Judson Press Publishers, 2021.

Keller, Timothy. *Center Church* Grand Rapids: Zondervan, 2012.

Kelley, Kitty. *His Way: An Unauthorized Biography of Frank Sinatra.,* New York: Random House Publishing, 2015.

Keyes, Sarah. *Like a Roaring Lion: The Overland Trail as a Sonic Quest.* Journal of American History 96, no.1 (2009), 19-43.

Kinnaman, David, and Mark Matlock. *Faith for Exiles: 5 Ways for a New Generation to Follow Jesus in Digital Babylon.* Grand Rapids. Baker Books, 2019.

Korkman, Petter. *Life, Liberty, and the Pursuit of Happiness.* In Transformation in Medieval and Early-Modern Rights Discourse, pp 25-283. Springer, Dordrecht, 2006.

Kornai, Janos. *Contradictions And Dilemmas: Studies on The Socialist Economy and Society.* Cambridge: MIT Press. 1986.

Kretchik, Walter Edward. *US Army Doctrine: From The American Revolution to The War on Terror*. Lawrence: University Press of Kansas, 2011.

Langston, Michael W., and Kathy J. Langston. *From Despair to Hope*. Silverton: Lampion Press, 2017.

Lehr, Fred. *Clergy Burnout, Revised and Expanded: Surviving in Turbulent Times* Minneapolis: Augsburg Fortress Publishers, 2022.

Levitas, Ruth. *For "Utopia: The (limits of) Utopian Function in Late Capitalist Society."* Critical Review of International Social and Political Philosophy 3, no. 2-3 (2000): 25-43.

Lewis, Clive Staples. *The Weight of Glory*, Grand Rapids: Zondervan, 2001.

──────────────. *The Problem of Pain*. New York: HarperCollins Publishers, 1996.

Lee, Moses Y. *"Who Is Melchizedek?"* Accessed December 20, 2022, https://thegospelcoalition.org/article/jesus-Melchizedek/.

MacArthur, John. *Fool's Gold?* Wheaton: Crossway Books, 2005.

Martin, Charles E. *"Dinner at the White House."* New York: Harper and Brothers. 1946. Pp 276. American Political Science Review 41, no. 3 (1947): 569-570.

Maynard, Dennis R. *When Sheep Attack!* USA: BookSurge Publishers, 2010.

Mayo Clinic Staff, *"Job Burnout: How to Spot It and Take Action – Mayo Clinic,"* Accessed November 2, 2022, https://www.mayoclinic.org/healthy-lifestyles/adult-health/in-debth/burnout/art-20046642.

McGrath, Alister. *Heresy: A History of Defending the Truth*. New York: Harper Collins Publishers, 2009.

McIntosh, Gary L., and Samuel D. Rima. *Overcoming the Dark Side of Leadership How to Become an Effective Leader by Confronting Potential Failures: Revised Edition,* Grand Rapids: Baker Books, 2007.

McLaren, Brian D. *A New Kind of Christianity – Ten Questions Transforming the Faith*. New York: Harper One, 2010.

McMinn, M. R., R. Allen Lish, Pamela D. Trice, Alicia M. Root, Nichole Gilbert, and Adelene Yap. *Care For Pastors: Learning from Clergy and Their Spouses*. Pastoral Psychology 53, no. 6 (2005): 563-581.

Mepkin Abbey, "*Mepkin Abbey.*" Accessed September 21, 2022. https://www.mepkinabbey.org/.

Merriam Webster. "*After-Action Report*" Accessed September 20, 2022, https://www.merriam-webster.com/dictionary/after-action%20report.

_____. "*Master Plan.*" Accessed September 23, 2022. https://www.merriam-webster.com/dictionary/master%20plan.

_____. "*No Man's Land,*" Accessed on November 30, 2022. https://www.merriam-webster.com/dictionary/no-man%27s-land.

Ministering to Ministers. Accessed May 20, 2023. https://ministeringtoministers.org/.

Montier, James. *The Little Book of Behavioral Investing: How Not to Be Your Worst Enemy, Vol. 35*. New Jersey: John Wiley & Sons. 2010

Music Therapy. Accessed June 2, 2023. https://www.psychologytoday.com/us/therapy-types/music-therapy.

Nagi, John A., James F. Amos, Sarah Sewall, and David H. Petraeus. *The US Army/ Marine Corps Counterinsurgency Field Manual.* Chicago: University of Chicago Press, 2009.

Newport, Frank. *The Gallop Poll. Public Opinion 2009.* Lanham: Rowman & Littlefield, 2009.

New Spring Church, "10 Bible Verses on Spiritual Warfare." Accessed December 12, 2022. https://newspring.cc/articles/10-scriptures-on-spiritual-warfare.

Nolland, John. *The Mandate: Love Our Enemies Matt. 5:43-48.* Anvil 21, no. 1 (2004): 23. Accessed April 20, 2023. https://biblicalstudies.org.uk.

Nouwen, Henri J. M. *The Wounded Healer Ministry in Contemporary Society,* New York: Random House Publishers, Inc., 1972.

_____. *The Wounded Healer Ministry in Contemporary Society.* New York: Random House Publishers, Inc., 1972.

Oxford Learner's Dictionary. "Concept," Accessed December 3, 2022. https://www.oxfordlearnersdictionaries.com/us/definition/american_english/concept#:~:text=concept-,noun,the%20basic%20concepts%20of%20mathematics.

Pastoral Care, Inc., *Statistics for Pastors,* Accessed December 15, 2022, https://www.pastoralcareinc.com/statistics.

Pattanaik, Binayak and Aditya Chauhan. *A Study of Stealth Technology.* Materials Today: Accessed May 3, 2023. https://www.sciencedirect.com > pii.

Pereira, Mary Ellen. *I Never Knew You: Jesus' Rebuke in Matthew 7:23.* Leaven 16, no. 4, 2008. Accessed April 17, 2023. https://digitalcommons.pepperdine.edu > …

Peterson, Eugene H. *"Curing Souls: The Forgotten Art,"* Accessed September 31, 2022, https://www.christianitytoday.com/pastors/1983/summer/8313048.

Pingleton, Jared P. *Why We Don't Forgive: A Biblical and Object Relations Theoretical Model for Understanding Failures in The Forgiveness Process.* Journal of Psychology and Theology 25, no. 4 (1997). 403-413.

Pope, Alexander, *An Essay on Man*, Accessed May 21, 2023. https://goodreads.com/quotes/10692-hope-springs-eternal-in-the-human-breast-man-never-is.

Proeschold-Bell, Rae-Jean and Jason Byassee. *Faithful and Fractured Responding to The Clergy Health Crisis,* Grand Rapids: Baker Academic, 2018.

Quesinberry, Kurtes D. *"Accessing Post-Traumatic Stress Disorder Care as a Resource for Pastoral Grief Counseling,"* TTGST Theological Journal, 12.1 (2009): 90-102.

Rape Crisis. *The 5 F's: Fight, Flight, Freeze, Flop, and Friend – Rape Crisis*, Accessed April 14, 2023, https://rapecrisis.org.UK > get-help.

Rediger, G. Lloyd. *Clergy Killers: Guidance for Pastors and Congregations Under Attack.* Louisville: Westminster John Knox Press, 1997.

_____. *Clergy Killers: Guidance for Pastors and Congregations Under Attack* Louisville: Westminster John Knox Press, 2001.

Richards, Larry. *Full Armor of God: Sandals of Peace.* Grand Rapids: Baker Books. 2013.

_____. *The Full Armor of God: Defending Your Life from Satan's Schemes.* Grand Rapids: Baker Books. 2013.

Roberts, Vaughn. *Workers for the Harvest Field.* Surrey UK: The Good Book Company, 2012.

Rohane, Kyle. *Christianity Today.* May/June 2022 Issue. Assessed June 21, 2023. https://christianitytoday.com.

Sacks, Jonathon. *Why Does God Allow Terrible Things to Happen to His People?* The Chesterton Review 34, no. ½ (2008): 367-370.

Scanlon, Christopher and Adlam, John. "Keep your friends close and your enemies closer." Sun-Tzu, Chinese military strategist (~ 400 BC) [1] This chapter is based on and adapted from a longer paper published in the journal Organizational and Social Dynamics, vol. 11 (2), pp. 175-195, under the title 'Who watches the watchers? Observing the dangerous liaisons." Accessed December 10, 2022.

Schimmel, Solomon. *The Seven Deadly Sins: Jewish, Christian, and Classical Reflections on Human Psychology.* Oxford: Oxford University Press, 1997.

Scott, Allen John. *On Hollywood: The Place, the Industry.* Princeton: Princeton University Press, 2005.

Silk, Mark. "*Notes on the Judeo-Christian tradition in America.*" American Quarterly, 36(1). Pp. 65-85. Accessed March 15, 2023.

Sinclair, Dean Thrift. "A New Town Will Appear on The Charleston Neck" Ph.D. diss., Louisiana State. University and Agricultura & Mechanical College, 2001. LSU Digital Commons (3042651).

Soul Shepherding Institute, "Soul Shepherding," Accessed November 6, 2022, https://www.soulshepherding.org/institute/.

Stewart, Anne W. *Moral Agency in The Hebrew Bible.* Accessed March 31, 2023. https://doi.org/10.1093/acrefore/9780199340378.013.92.2016.

Tada, Joni Eareckson, and Steven Estes. *"When God Weeps,"* Grand Rapids: Zondervan, 1997.

Talmon, Yonia. *Family and Community in The Kibbutz.* Vol. 67. Cambridge: Harvard University Press, 1972.

Tanner, Paul. *"The Cost of Discipleship: Losing One's Life for Jesus' Sake."* Journal of the Evangelical Theological Society 56, no. 1 (2013): 43.

Taylor, Joan E., *"Golgotha: A Reconsideration of The Evidence for The Sites of Jesus' Crucifixion and Burial."* New Testament Studies 44, no 2 (1998): 180-203.

The Editors of Encyclopedia Britannica. *Seven Deadly Sins Definition, History, Names, & Examples.* Accessed October 23, 2022, https://Britannica.com/seven_deadly_sins. hmtl.

The Healing Benefits of Art Therapy. Accessed May 25, 2023. https://sageclinic.org/blog/healing-art-therapy/.

The Indigo Project. *"Our Four Greatest Fears (And What They Say About Us),"* Accessed April 14, 2023, https://www.theindigoproject.com.

History Channel. "The Reformation," Accessed March 11, 2023. https://www.history.com>topics>reformation.

The Voice of the Martyrs. Accessed April 12, 2023. https://www.persecution.com.

Tickle, Phyllis. *"The Great Emergence: How Christianity is Changing and Why."* Kentwood: Baker Books, 2012.

Tighe, Michael W. *"Role of the Secretary of State under the South Carolina Business Corporation Act of 1962,"* South Carolina Law

Review, 15, no. 2 (1963): 15. https://scholarcommons.sc.edu/cgi/viewcontent.cgi?article=1623&context=sclr.

Torrey, Charles C. "*Armageddon.*" Harvard Theological Review 31, no. 3 (1938): 237-248.

Treier, Daniel J. and Anizor, Uche. *Theological Interpretation of Scripture and Evangelical Systematic Theology: Iron Sharpening Iron.* Southern Baptist Journal of Theology 14 (2010): 4-17.

Abigail Van Buren, "*Goodreads,*" https://www.goodreads.c/quotes, Accessed October 31, 2022.

Vanderveen, Julia Prins. "*A Heart of Stone - Today Daily Devotional,*" Accessed November 22, 2022. https://todaydevotional.com/devotions/a-heart-of-stone.

Wazana, Nili. *All the Boundaries of The Land: The Promised Land in Biblical Thought in Light of The Ancient Near East.* University Park: Penn State Press, 2013, 185.

Webb, Jonice, Ph.D., *Why Grief Is a Breeding Ground for Guilt,* Psychology Today, Accessed November 30, 2022. https://www.psychologytoday.com/s/blog/childhood-emotional-neglect/202210/why-grief-is-breeding-ground-guilt.

Wiesel, Elie. *Night.* New York: Hill and Wang, 2017.

Witherington III, Ben. *Jesus, Paul, and the End of the World.* Westmont: Intervarsity Press, 1992.

Wright, H. Norman. *Helping Those in Grief. What to Say and What Not to Say. A Guide to Help You Care for Others,* Ventura: Regal from Gospel Light, 2010.

Yadin, Azzan. *Goliath's Armor and Israelite's Collective Memory.* Vetus Testamentum 54, no. 3 (2004). 373-395.

Yeazell, Stephen C. *Meeting the Enemy.* DePaul L. Rev. 50 (2000-2001): 667.

Yehuda, Rachael. "Post-Traumatic Stress Disorder." New England Journal of Medicine. 346, no. 2 (2002): 108-114.

Zizek, Slavoj. *Living in the End Times.* Brooklyn: Verso Books. 2011.